EVERYDAY
MIRACLES

EVERYDAY MIRACLES

TRUE STORIES ABOUT GOD'S HAND IN OUR LIVES

JAY A. PARRY

EAGLE
GATE

Library of Congress Cataloging-in-Publication Data

Parry, Jay A.
  Everyday miracles / Jay A. Parry.
    p.   cm.
  ISBN 1-57008-777-6 (pbk.)
    1. Christian life—Mormon authors. 2. Miracles. I. Title.
BX8656 .P365 2001
248.4'89332—dc21   2001003001

Printed in the United States of America   72082-6907

10   9   8   7   6   5   4   3   2   1

CONTENTS

Introduction xi

"Cast Your Bread . . . "
CARMA N. CUTLER 1

Every Day He Would Irritate Me
EMILY J. RAWSON 4

They Lived on Ice Cream Cones
MARY ANN STRONG 6

Rescue That Boy
LELAND E. ANDERSON 9

I Prayed Again for Strength
SARAH JANE WIGHT 12

Why Would God Help Me?
ARDETH G. KAPP 15

I Was Determined to Forget about Joseph Smith
CAROLYN J. RASMUS 17

I Doubted My Worth
JULIE STINSON BLACK 21

"Arise and Be Baptized"
AUTHOR UNKNOWN 23

CONTENTS

"Sunshine in My Soul"
GARRICK GREENHALGH 27

Stuck in a Stream
CINDEE KEISER 31

I Didn't Feel Peace As a Wife and Mother
JODY HIGHAM PIERCE 33

Two Bags of Cement
JOHN PURSER 38

"Have You Considered Everyone?"
R. REED CHANNELL 40

"My Burden Is Light"
DAVID C. HOLBROOK 42

Leave for West Berlin Today
DIETER BERNDT 45

He Wrapped Her Legs in Hot Towels
DEE ANN BARROWES 50

The Spirit Teaches Scripture
JEAN ASAY 52

He Found Us on the Map
EVA DAWN JONES 55

God Give Me Strength!
BLAINE RASMUSSEN 58

The Lord Had Promised His Help
R. SAMUEL RIRIE 60

I Was Unable to Read Even One Name
JOAN LLOYD HOFHEINS 62

The Lord Was Ready
CHRISTIE ANN GILES 67

. . . Until They Know We Care
ROBERT L. MILLET 69

I Applied on the Last Day
JOHN J. MCINTYRE 74

Not Open on Sunday!
QUINTEN AND LARAE WARR, AS TOLD TO RUTH HEINER 77

I Wanted One More Summer of Fun
TREVOR SANDBERG 80

A Mother's Prayer
DARLENE SANDBERG 84

I Prayed That My Burdens Would Be Light
TRISHA GORDON 88

"Stop and See Your Dad"
JOHN W. MARKHAM 92

The Lord Gave Me My Jobs
SUZANNE FENSTERMAKER 95

What Can I Do to Be Happy?
ALLAN K. BURGESS AND MAX H. MOLGARD 98

The Contact Lens
RICHARD H. CRACROFT 101

CONTENTS

He Showed Me My Hidden Weaknesses
REBEKAH ISAACSON 105

The Light That Leadeth Me Back
LAUREN A. DICK 107

"You Already Know"
TANDEA FORD 112

The Signals the Doctors Needed
RICHARD T. SOWELL 114

We Rushed Him to the Hospital
J. C. AARONS 117

"Adams, How Do You Do It?"
PETER C. ADAMS 119

She Dug the Grave with Her Fingers
FREDERICK W. BABBEL 124

Deliverance from a Cliff
ORLANDO T. BARRROWES 127

God and I Were of One Mind
BONNIE BALLIF-SPANVILL 129

"Don't Go into Times Square!"
ALDEN PERKES 132

Only God Gives A's
BRETT G. LONDON 135

Nothing Seemed to Help
TRACEY GRIFFIN 138

I Stepped Off the Bridge
  ATWELL J. PARRY 140

All I Had Prayed For
  JoANN TAYLOR 143

Keys to Peace
  TAMARA JOLIE 146

The Lord's Gift of Love
  DANIEL A. TOLMAN 148

We Called a Family Fast
  BRANDON R. WILLIAMS 151

"Go into Another Room"
  JOYCE LINDSTROM 153

Trust the Path I Walk
  DEBRA SANSING WOODS 155

It Sold on the Last Day
  THOMAS R. CLARK 161

The Gas Gauge Was Below Empty
  JENNA LEE 164

A Prayer on the Run
  JON M. TAYLOR 167

The Road Back Home
  MARGARET BARTON WILSON 170

It Felt Like Walking into a Wall
  MICHAEL EARL 185

CONTENTS

A Warmth Washed over Me

JUDY TAYLOR YOUNG 187

A Night of Fires

GEORGE C. THORDERSEN 189

"Do You Remember the Promises You Made?

FREDERICK W. BABBEL 191

One Chance at Law School

WENDY D. YOUNG 195

One Shovelful of Coal

MARJORIE A. MCCORMICK 198

Sources 201

Scripture Index 203

Index 205

About the Author 213

INTRODUCTION

Ours is a gospel of miracles. In his love and power, our Father in Heaven grants to his children special dispensations of grace, unique blessings, to help them face (and sometimes conquer) the challenges of mortal life.

Some miracles are called "mighty miracles" (2 Nephi 10:4; Mosiah 3:5; 8:18; Moroni 10:12). These would include such miracles as the plagues that came upon Egypt through the priesthood declarations of Moses, moving mountains and dividing seas, raising the dead, giving sight to the blind and hearing to the deaf, converting a nation in a day, feeding five thousand people with a few loaves and fishes, and so forth. Such miracles are rare—some would occur only once in a generation, or once in a dispensation, or even less frequently than that.

But most miracles the Lord gives us might be termed "everyday miracles." Each week we have the opportunity to renew sacred covenants as we partake of the sacrament. The Lord's promise is that his Spirit will always be with us as we keep those covenants (D&C 20:77, 79). A natural consequence of that companionship of the Spirit is a continuing series of small miracles—whisperings of guidance and protection, strengthened and renewed testimonies, comfort and peace, gifts of love and joy.

As we seek the Lord with true desire, he will send answers to our prayers. If we seek the blessing, he will help us come to a broken heart, gain power over our thoughts and habits, and develop deepened spiritual understandings. He will help us in relationships with loved ones and with problems in the temporal world. Sometimes he will grant us healing from a physical or emotional ailment. Sometimes he will give us strength to endure that ailment.

Each of these blessings is a manifestation of godly power in our lives, and any such manifestation is, by definition, a miracle (see Bible Dictionary, "Miracles").

"These signs shall follow them that believe," the Lord said. "In my name shall they cast out devils; they shall speak with new tongues; they shall take up serpents; and if they drink any deadly thing, it shall not hurt them: they shall lay hands on the sick, and they shall recover" (Mark 16:17–18). Knowing what we do of divine declarations in other scriptures, we might appropriately add to the list by saying, These signs shall also follow them that believe:

In the world, though they have tribulation, they shall be of good cheer, and the Lord will console them in their afflictions (John 16:33; Jacob 3:1).

In their time of trouble, the Lord will "speak peace" to their souls (Alma 58:11).

"All things shall work together for [their] good" (D&C 90:24).

God will grant that their "burdens may be light, through the joy of his Son" (Alma 33:23).

They will "suffer no manner of afflictions, save it [be] swallowed up in the joy of Christ" (Alma 31:38).

The Lord will "make them mighty even unto the power of deliverance" (1 Nephi 1:20).

They will live "after the manner of happiness" (2 Nephi 5:27).

The Spirit will enlighten their minds and fill their souls with joy (D&C 11:13).

They will "not be tempted above that which [they] can bear" (Alma 13:28).

They will "be able to quench all the fiery darts of the wicked" (Ephesians 6:16).

The Lord will "direct [them] for good" (Alma 37:37).

The Lord will lead them by the hand, and give them answer to their prayers (D&C 112:10).

They will receive "instruction of [God's] Spirit" (D&C 6:14).

They will "receive revelation upon revelation, knowledge upon knowledge, . . . the mysteries and peaceable things" (D&C 42:61).

They "shall know the truth, and the truth shall make [them] free" (John 8:32).

The Lord will "nourish them, and strengthen them, and provide means whereby they can accomplish the thing which he has commanded them" (1 Nephi 17:3).

The Lord will baptize them "with fire and with the Holy Ghost" (3 Nephi 9:20).

They will "always retain a remission of [their] sins" (Mosiah 4:12).

They will "be filled with the love of God," insomuch that the Lord will encircle them in the arms of his love (Mosiah 4:12; D&C 6:20).

These are miracles, every one, granted by a gracious God who loves us and seeks from day to day to bless in ways both great and small.

Some will ask, What of those with faith who aren't healed, who don't have a protecting prompting, whose wayward children don't come back, who pay tithing and don't receive material help in time of need, who pray and desperately needed blessings still don't come? There are indeed many such instances in the Church, and they can indeed happen with people of faith. The answer to these difficult questions could fill an entire book and more, but perhaps it will be sufficient here to say that those in such circumstances can receive their own miracles, suited to their needs by a God who knows best what mortal experiences will help them on their way to godhood—they can receive blessings of comfort in trial; they can receive loving reminders from the Spirit that God remembers them even in their time of distress, even though deliverance from their afflictions may not be part of the divine design. And they can rejoice with those who have been delivered, and can reach out with understanding hearts to minister to others who have not.

MORE THAN COINCIDENCE

"Have miracles ceased because Christ hath ascended into heaven?" Mormon asked, and then answered his own question: "Behold I say unto you, Nay; for it is by faith that miracles are wrought; . . . wherefore, if these things have ceased wo be unto the children of men, for it is because of unbelief, and all is vain. . . . But behold, my beloved brethren, I judge better things of you, for I judge that ye have faith in Christ because of your meekness" (Moroni 7:27, 37, 39).

Of course, miracles have not ceased. God is manifesting his power in our lives from day to day, working a quiet work in and through us that gives us a constant reminder that he is near and that he loves us. President Spencer W. Kimball wrote:

"A question often asked is: If miracles are a part of the gospel program, why do we not have such today?

"The answer is a simple one: We do have miracles today— beyond imagination! If all the miracles of our own lifetime were recorded, it would take many library shelves to hold the books which would contain them.

"What kinds of miracles do we have? All kinds—revelations, visions, tongues, healings, special guidance and direction, evil spirits cast out. Where are they recorded? In the records of the Church, in journals, in news and magazine articles and in the minds and memories of many people" (*Teachings of Spencer W. Kimball*, 499).

Unfortunately, small miracles are sometimes so subtle, or so common, that they may be overlooked. Elder Jay E. Jensen relates this helpful experience with the workings of the Spirit:

"As a branch president at the Missionary Training Center in Provo, Utah, I have heard several missionaries say in their initial interviews that they did not have testimonies or that they could never remember a time when they had had a spiritual experience. After talking about how the Spirit works, they realized that they had, in fact, had a number of spiritual experiences but had not realized it before.

"Perhaps this lack of awareness is fostered in part by hearing or reading about spectacular spiritual experiences. Frequent exposure to such experiences may lead some to believe that if they haven't experienced some similar kind of outpouring or manifestation, they haven't had a spiritual experience" ("Have I Received an Answer from the Spirit?" *Ensign*, April 1989, 21).

Another typical response to certain types of everyday miracles is to see them simply as coincidences. Was a person healed because of faith and a priesthood blessing, or because of the natural healing processes of the body? When a blessing comes after seeking it in prayer, was the prayer an active ingredient in the process? The answer to such queries is that miracles always lie in the realm of faith, and that the Spirit can testify to the person having the experience (and the person hearing it) whether or not the experience was of God.

To those who doubt the small workings of the Lord, Moroni warns, "Dispute not because ye see not" (Ether 12:6); and he seems to have reference even to small miracles when he asks, "Who will despise the works of the Lord?" (Mormon 9:26). With Jacob, then, we say, "Wherefore, brethren, despise not the revelations of God" (Jacob 4:8)—even when he reveals himself in ways that are quiet and small. After all, as Nephi wrote, "By small means the Lord can bring about great things" (1 Nephi 16:29). God spoke to Elijah (the earthly agent of many mighty miracles) not in the "great and strong wind," not in the earthquake, not in the fire, but in the "still small voice" (1 Kings 19:11–12).

"I have not heard angels sing like my grandmother did," says Sister Marjorie Pay Hinckley, "nor have I witnessed any other spectacular miracle. And I am grateful. My testimony has been fed by small, simple, and sometimes seemingly unimportant experiences. I think this is as it should be. There are very few big and spectacular miracles in most of our lives. But it is a quiet multitude of little miracles that makes life sweet and adds to our testimonies" (*Glimpses into the Life and Heart of Marjorie Pay Hinckley*, 204–5).

Those are the kind of miracles represented in the pages of this book. Of course, the stories told here are not of everyday experiences in each of our lives. But they are everyday occurrences in the Church. No, someone isn't warned to stay out of Times Square each day, or healed after being kicked in the head by a horse. But it *is* an everyday miracle in the Church for people to be warned by the Spirit, or to be healed. So it is with all the miracles shared here: they are the kind of things that are happening daily in the lives of the Lord's people.

Because miracles and spiritual experiences are by nature personal and sacred, many are not appropriate for publication. They are to be kept and pondered in one's heart, or perhaps told privately and in a limited basis to family members or to selected others as prompted by the Spirit (see D&C 63:64; Alma 12:9). Even those experiences that may appropriately be shared (particularly on a public forum such as a book or talk) should sometimes be done so anonymously, that we may rejoice in the goodness of God without any hint or suggestion of boasting or of setting oneself up as a model for others. We have accordingly changed the names of a number of the authors of the stories in this book (using a pseudonym, with their encouragement and permission), and sometimes have changed such details as time and place, without changing the story itself.

Finally, there are many stories in Mormon culture that might be classified as "Mormon myths," or "Mormon urban legends." We have sought carefully to include only stories that are true, stories that actually happened to the person recounting them or that have been related to them by the one who had the experience. We have also chosen to avoid those stories that might be termed spectacular (though many such may also be true). In this category would fall stories involving angels and other heavenly visitors (except those who remain unseen), the gift of tongues, raising people from the dead, understanding the deeper mysteries of the gospel, and so forth. Though such experiences certainly qualify as miracles, their very nature suggests that they cannot be called "everyday miracles."

I would like to thank the many people who helped to gather, record, and type the stories in this book. Particularly helpful were Dee Ann E. Barrowes, Norma Barrowes, Tandea Ford, Latrisha Gordon, Bonnie Lee McIntyre, Atwell J. Parry, Elaine Parry, and Vicki L. Parry. I also thank those whose stories were previously published elsewhere for their gracious permission to reprint them here. Finally, I want to thank the publishing staff at Deseret Book for their excellent and professional work. I express gratitude to all those who made significant contributions to the creation of this book, including Sheri Dew, Jana Erickson, Janna DeVore, Tom Hewitson, and Laurie Cook.

Cast thy bread upon the waters:
for thou shalt find it after many days.

ECCLESIASTES 11:1

"CAST YOUR BREAD . . ."
CARMA N. CUTLER

Among the many wonderful people we met when we lived in a small town in Utah years ago was a family named Williams. They were a good family of strong faith and testimony. But Brother and Sister Williams had five small children and struggled to make ends meet. Then Brother Williams' back was broken in an automobile accident, and he was hospitalized for several weeks.

As counselor in our ward Relief Society presidency, I went with our president to visit Sister Williams and her young family. What a blessing the Church welfare program is at a time like this! As our president explained how the program worked, Sister Williams was relieved of many anxieties.

When I arrived home, I couldn't get the plight of this young mother out of my mind. I could identify with her because we had six young children at home, and they really kept me busy. I kept wondering what I personally could do for her. My thoughts went to milk. I was sure her family drank milk by the gallons, as mine did, and we had found a dairy that sold milk cheaper than the stores or home delivery. I called Sister Williams about it, and she told me she got her milk there too, so I arranged to get hers when I went for mine. When I went to pick up her cans, she had them and the money ready for me, but I told her I would like to buy her milk that day. She resisted, but finally relented.

I went back a couple of days later to get her cans again, but she was hesitant—she didn't have any money. I told her not to worry, that I wanted to buy the milk for her. This arrangement went on for several weeks, until I began to feel the strain on my own budget and found myself borrowing money from my children.

But just as I decided I would have to tell Sister Williams that I could no longer buy her milk, I noticed that every "milk day" some little miracle would happen. I remember one day there simply was no extra money and I was ready to reach for the phone when I was prompted to go to the mailbox first. I did; and there was a little check—just enough for the milk—for some jury duty I had performed earlier in the year. I continued to buy milk.

One evening several weeks later Brother Williams was released from the hospital. He was in a brace, but he insisted on coming by our home to thank us personally for buying their milk. However, their compensation checks were coming in now, and everything was going to be all right for them.

After they left, I leaned against the door and silently thanked the Lord that I had never told Sister Williams I couldn't get her milk. Still, that very day I had only had enough money to buy their milk, but not ours; and our littlest, Chuck, would be awake at six o'clock next morning, wanting a drink.

The very next morning, before Chuck was even awake, there came a knock on our door. On the step stood a young man from our ward holding two big jugs of milk. He said, "Sister Cutler, I understand you have a big family. For some reason or other our cow has started giving more milk than we can use, and we just hate pouring it down the sink. Would you be insulted if I dropped it off here each morning on my way to work?"

I couldn't believe it! Immediately, into my mind flashed a saying I had heard my mother quote often when I was a little girl: "Cast your bread upon the waters, and after many days it will return—buttered" (see Ecclesiastes 11:1). By the time that cow got back to normal production, we had received two or three times more milk than we had ever given away.

"Cast Your Bread . . . ," Carma N. Cutler. Previously published in the *Ensign*, June 1981, 70–71. © by Intellectual Reserve, Inc. Used by permission.

Charity suffereth long, and . . . is not easily provoked.

1 CORINTHIANS 13:4–5

EVERY DAY HE WOULD IRRITATE ME
EMILY J. RAWSON

The year after I graduated from high school, I started working for my dad in his small business office. I would spend at least half of my time working directly with him on many and detailed projects.

I loved my dad, but I dreaded going to work. All day, every day, he would do little things in the office that would irritate me. He wouldn't listen the first three times I said his name. He would tell me that I was too slow or not organizing the work well enough. He would mumble directions so that I couldn't understand. He would wave away papers that I was trying to hand to him if he didn't want them. Every little, irritating thing he would do would trouble me until, at the end of the day, I would be absolutely emotionally and physically exhausted.

It came to a head for me one day when he criticized me about something and I broke down crying. I couldn't handle it anymore.

I didn't want to work for him, but I knew that he needed me. In addition, I had prayed about it more than once and felt that the Lord wanted me to stay.

Finally I went to the Lord again in prayer. I didn't feel that I could quit, but I did feel that he would help me make it better. Through much prayer and opening myself to the blessing, I learned that the way to make working for my dad better was not to change my dad, but to change myself.

Through the Spirit, the Lord told me that I was harboring feelings of anger for my dad. I was angry at him for things he had done in the past and for some things he was presently doing that I didn't agree with—but not necessarily for things he did at work. The Lord helped me to recognize these angry feelings, let go of them, and forgive my dad.

It took a long time for me to fully work through, reject, and let go of the anger. I had to pray every time I felt the feelings come back, which was several times a day. I know that it was the atonement of Jesus Christ that changed me. While my dad still did all the same things, they didn't irritate me. I was freed from the burden of anger.

*If it so be that the children of men keep the
commandments of God he doth nourish them,
and strengthen them, and provide means
whereby they can accomplish the thing
which he has commanded them.*

1 NEPHI 17:3

THEY LIVED ON ICE CREAM CONES
MARY ANN STRONG

When my father was six years old his mother died. It was during the great flu epidemic of 1918, and she was selfless in her service to those who were afflicted. With no concern for her own health, she had served the sick until she became ill herself and died, leaving a heartbroken husband and five children, two boys and three girls. My dad was the second youngest.

The family struggled but remained strong. Then tragedy struck again when, eight years later, the faithful husband and father also passed away. Well-meaning relatives wanted to break up the children and distribute them among the aunts. But the children were determined to stay together, and they vowed that they would live alone and care for each other.

One day some years later, my dad and his brother were working in a field for a neighbor as hired hands. The bishop of the ward came by and asked them why they didn't go on full-time missions. They responded that they had no one to support them.

As they considered their deep desire to serve, my father and his brother made a pact. They agreed that first my uncle would accept a mission call, and my father would work to support him. In return, when my uncle came home, my father would go on a mission and be supported by my uncle.

The older brother received a call to serve in California. The younger brother, my father, worked hard and was able to support him for his entire mission. Then it was my dad's turn. He also received a call to serve in California.

His brother worked and sent money for a while, but soon he fell in love and got married. His wife became pregnant and was terribly sick. It was all my uncle could do to work and care for his home and his very ill wife. He could no longer support my father.

For two months my father and his companion visited an ice cream store and asked for their broken, rejected cones. These cones were their primary food for those months because my father had no money.

After weeks of subsisting on the damaged cones, it became apparent to my father that he could not continue on his mission without financial help. He decided to share his dilemma with his mission president. Unfortunately, the president had no funds to draw on at that time and was unable to offer any help.

Because of his desire to finish his mission, my dad fasted and prayed, asking Heavenly Father to help him know what to do. It wasn't long after that the mission president contacted him and told him the following story:

A member of the Church from Los Angeles had contacted the mission headquarters and told the president that her son had saved sufficient money to support himself on a mission; then, just before he was old enough to go, he had died. She wanted to send the money to support a needy missionary so that the funds would be used as her son had intended.

The mission president asked my father if he would like to receive sufficient money every month from this lady and her son's mission fund. My father was overwhelmed and thankful. This indeed was an answer to his pleadings. He was sustained for the remainder of his mission, always thankful that he could complete his time of service.

The effectual fervent prayer of a righteous man availeth much.

JAMES 5:16

RESCUE THAT BOY
LELAND E. ANDERSON

One evening when I was serving as stake president in Manti, Utah, Brother Roscoe Eardley of Salt Lake City, a member of the Church Welfare Committee, stayed at our home. He related the following memorable story to us:

He was returning home from a welfare meeting late one evening, going east on Fourth South Street in Salt Lake City. As he approached Main Street, he noticed a soldier and a young woman walking along the street, with the young woman seeming to pull her companion along with her. Brother Eardley smiled to himself as he passed them. But when he had gone about half a block further, he seemed to hear a voice say to him, "Brother Eardley, turn your car around and go back and rescue that young man from that woman."

He did not hesitate; he about-faced and soon was pulling up to the side of the street where the woman was still pulling the soldier along with her.

Brother Eardley jumped out of his car, went up to them both, and said, "Young lady, I am sorry, but this man is my prisoner. You will just have to give him to me." She objected strenuously, but soon Brother Eardley had the soldier in his car with him and the woman went on down the street crying.

As they drove along, the soldier explained that he was stationed at Fort Douglas, a military reservation east of Salt Lake City. When asked how he happened to be in the company of a woman of questionable morals, he explained, "Tonight, for some reason, I felt very lonely up at the Fort, and I thought I would go downtown to see if I could find something to cheer me up. I had heard that the Mormons were wonderful people and that this was a good town. As I was walking down Main Street, I heard jazzy music being played below in a basement room. I just went down the stairway and found a dancing party going on. I stood and watched for a few minutes, when a couple came up to me and asked me to join them. So I did."

He recalled that it wasn't long until he wished he had stayed at the Fort. Liquor was flowing freely at the party and he soon found himself inebriated. Then the young woman approached him and suggested they get some fresh air. He soon found her urging him on, but he was too drunk to realize what was happening. That was when Brother Eardley came by and rescued him.

Brother Eardley took him to his home, helped revive his spirits as best he could, and asked him to spend the night there. The soldier declined, however, as he noticed with alarm that he was due back at Fort Douglas in an hour. Brother Eardley drove him back to the Fort. He also assured the young man that the Mormon people *were* some of the best people on earth, and that Salt Lake

City was a fine place in which to live. He insisted that the soldier come to spend the next weekend with the Eardley family.

When he arrived at Brother Eardley's home that weekend, the soldier had dinner with the family, who then showed him around the city. He was invited to spend each weekend with this gracious family.

About two weeks later the soldier arrived, almost out of breath. He had news from his family in Pennsylvania. "Mr. Eardley," he said, "I want you to read a letter from my mother."

In the letter, the mother told her son about a terrible dream she had had a few nights before. She named the night, and it was the very night Brother Eardley had met the young man downtown. She said she woke up suddenly and saw in a sort of vision that her son was in great danger.

She got down on her knees and pleaded with the Lord to save her son. In noting the time this took place, Brother Eardley discovered that the woman was praying for her son at the exact time a voice told him, "Go back and rescue that boy."

What a wonderful letter! Jesus said, "For he that is not against us is on our part" (Mark 9:40). He told Peter and his other followers not to stop people from doing good, for it would all rebound to the good of the Church (Mark 9:38–41). We are all of one parenthood—children of the Father. He answers the sincere, earnest prayer. May we each live lives of such merit that we can entertain revelations, as Brother Eardley did, and walk within the light of that which is revealed to us.

Anderson, *Stories of Power and Purpose*, 52.

*Inasmuch as ye have done it unto one of the least
of these my brethren, ye have done it unto me.*

MATTHEW 25:40

I PRAYED AGAIN FOR STRENGTH
SARAH JANE WIGHT

When I served as a ward Relief Society president, I felt the weight of the assignment, but also felt that things were going fairly well. Our ward had a strong organization with good teachers and a stable visiting teaching program. Our homemaking meetings were helpful, and our special occasions were well attended and lovely, with pleasing decorations and good food.

I had things well in hand. I was able to delegate effectively and keep things running quite smoothly.

One day I received a call from a member of my ward who seemed very distressed. This good brother was caring for his aged mother at his home. He had no help from other family members. The burden was heavy, but as far as I knew he had been doing all right. His voice cracked as he told me his plight on the telephone.

He said that his mother had gone into a coma-like state three days before. She had not eaten or awakened. The doctors had advised him that there was no purpose in taking her to the hospital, since her death was imminent. He had stayed by her bedside for those three days. But he was not able to bring himself to care for her very personal needs. This was his mother, a shy and reserved little woman from the old country. Out of respect for her lifelong practice of modesty and privacy, he simply could not remove her soiled clothing or wash her in any of the places she most needed washing.

He said that he didn't know what to do. Could I send a sister from the ward to help him with her? I reassured him that help would come.

I made many, many calls. Usually my attempts to get help were answered with positive results. I was a good delegator and had a good ward. But this time I was not able to find one woman who could go to that home. What was I to do? I was a fairly good Relief Society president, but I usually left things like this to a person's family or friends or to the visiting teachers. I came to the realization that I must go myself.

The man greeted me at his door with gratitude in his eyes. He led me to his mother's bedroom and opened the door. I couldn't believe what I saw. There lay a little old woman in her own body wastes. She had matted hair. She didn't move. Her chest rattled when she breathed her shallow breath. The smell in the room was so bad I almost couldn't enter.

I sent a quick prayer upward and asked the man for warm water, a towel, a washcloth, and some soap. I also wanted him to get some clean sheets and another gown for his mother. He gathered the things I needed. Then I excused him, entered the room, and shut the door.

I almost fainted. I prayed again for strength.

Just as I was about to begin, these words came very clearly into my mind: "Inasmuch as ye have done it unto one of the least of these my brethren, ye have done it unto me."

My heart was touched and changed. It was in that very moment that I turned into a good Relief Society president. I learned the meaning of charity that day.

I washed my sister with the gentle touch of love and caring. I cleaned her body and brushed her hair. I changed her sheets and her clothes. And all the while I felt the privilege of doing it. I left with the unending gratitude from a dutiful son, but it was I who had received the blessing.

The next day, my dear sister passed away. She died in the comfort of a clean bed and with the dignity she deserved. And my attitude about service, in every capacity, had been changed forever.

He remembereth every creature of his creating.

MOSIAH 27:30

WHY WOULD GOD HELP ME?
ARDETH G. KAPP

I felt God's presence in a letter received not too long ago from a young man who is an inmate in the state prison. He wrote:

"I couldn't understand what interest God would have in someone like me, for I was a drug addict and convicted felon who hadn't prayed or gone to church in almost ten years. Still the feeling persisted, and even intensified, until one afternoon I finally was drawn to my knees in prayer in the privacy of my steel and concrete prison cell. For perhaps the first time ever I opened my heart to God. I said, 'Heavenly Father, I know that you are there, but I don't know why. Why would you want to help someone such as me?' And the answer came softly, but so clearly and deeply felt that I've never been able to think about it without feeling it once again and having tears come to my eyes. 'Mark, it is because I love you.' How inexpressibly wonderful it felt to know that the God of the universe knew me and loved me. I stayed on my knees praying and crying for hours, and from that day on, I was truly a changed person. Not only was my heart changed, but my entire life was changed. With God's help, old habits can be overcome."

Kapp, *The Joy of the Journey*, 171.

The Spirit giveth light to every man that cometh into the world;
and the Spirit enlighteneth every man through the world,
that hearkeneth to the voice of the Spirit.

D&C 84:46

I WAS DETERMINED TO FORGET ABOUT JOSEPH SMITH

CAROLYN J. RASMUS

[Several months after hearing of the gospel] I decided to fast for the first time in my life. It was a day when I was also studying for a statistics test. I was unsettled and unable to concentrate on studying for the test. Finally, I knelt down to pray. I have no rec-ollection of the prayer I offered, but these thoughts came into my mind and I felt impressed to record them on a scrap of paper:

"October 12, 1970, 8:45 A.M. Go now, my child, for there is much work to be done. I send my Spirit to be with you to enable you to work and think clearly, to accomplish all that lies before you this day. Go now and know that I am with you in all things, and later return to me, coming to me with real intent of prayer. Know that I am the Lord, that all things are possible to them who call upon my name. Take comfort in these words. Fill your heart with joy and gladness, not sorrow and despair. Lo, I am with you always, even unto the end of the world. Know me as Comforter and Savior."

That evening I wanted to be alone. I went to my student office on campus, locked the door, turned out the lights, and prayed. I wanted answers to the questions I'd been asking. I didn't expect an angel to appear, but I wanted some kind of manifestation that would prove, once and for all, that these things were true or false.

Nothing happened! The experience earlier in the day had no particular meaning because I did not yet understand what Enos taught, that the voice of the Lord can come into our mind (see Enos 1:10). I also knew nothing about the principle of learning "by *study* and also by *faith*" (D&C 88:118). Now I recognize I was like Oliver Cowdery in that I "supposed that [God] would give it unto [me], when [I] took no thought save it was to ask" (D&C 9:7).

I left my office determined to forget about Joseph Smith, the Book of Mormon, and everything associated with The Church of Jesus Christ of Latter-day Saints. But I couldn't. These things seemed to be constantly on my mind. Several months later I had the impression that I should begin to pay tithing. For more than three months, each time I received a paycheck I took 10 percent of my meager student teacher wage and put the cash in a white envelope carefully hidden in a dresser drawer. I never had a desire to touch the money or to use it for something else. Although I wasn't sure how to give it to him, I believed it belonged to the Lord. I did other things that seemed and felt right. I would attend the Lutheran Church in the morning and then go with friends to sacrament meeting and Sunday School. I stopped drinking coffee, which had always seemed harmless to me and which I had never understood was part of the honor code I had promised to keep when I enrolled at BYU. I spent many hours helping a friend memorize the missionary discussions before she left for her mission.

I believe I felt impressed to do these things because "the Spirit giveth light to every man that cometh into the world; and the Spirit enlighteneth every man through the world, that hearkeneth to the voice of the Spirit" (D&C 84:46). Elder Bruce R. McConkie explains, "It is this spirit that leads men to accept the gospel and join the Church so that they may receive the gift of the Holy Ghost" (*Mormon Doctrine* [Salt Lake City: Bookcraft, 1966], 447).

Only two weeks before I would join the Church, I sat in a sacrament meeting and the following words came pounding into my head: "Know that Joseph Smith was a prophet and that through him my Church has been restored in these latter days. Know that the Book of Mormon is the word of God. Know that my Church has been reestablished upon the earth in these latter days. Know that I intend for you to be baptized. Know, believe, do."

These thoughts went through my head day and night for a week. The next Sunday during the sacrament service as I passed the bread to my neighbor, another thought came into my mind: "How much longer can you pass by the bread of life?" Six days later, on March 6, 1971, I was baptized and became a member of The Church of Jesus Christ of Latter-day Saints.

Within a week of my baptism, I received a letter dated March 6 from a friend who was serving a mission in Brazil. She wrote: "It's 11:20 here in São Paulo, 7:20 there in Provo. I should be in bed, but for some reason I have a deep desire to visit with you. You have been in my thoughts, especially today. My thoughts won't let me rest in peace until I write." After telling me of her missionary work, she bore her testimony and concluded, "The unyielding need to communicate with you has been satisfied, and I am ready to go to bed. I go in peace knowing this is a special day, and we have shared together for a few moments."

Shortly I learned that my letter to her, mailed within an hour following my baptism, arrived in São Paulo on the day I received her letter. She wrote telling me that when she received my letter she told her companion before opening it, "This will be the letter telling me that my friend has joined the Church."

My experience with these letters taught me an important principle—the Spirit has power to communicate things in ways we do not understand. As is so often the case in our daily lives, events and circumstances that seem so ordinary and commonplace at the time of their happening take on deeper meaning in retrospect.

Rasmus, *In the Strength of the Lord I Can Do All Things*, 5–9.

Look unto God with firmness of mind,
and pray unto him with exceeding faith,
and he will console you in your afflictions.

JACOB 3:1

I DOUBTED MY WORTH
JULIE STINSON BLACK

I grew up in a family with four older brothers. My father was a good man in many ways but he was very opinionated and filled with pride. In contrast to my assertive and confident brothers and father, I was very timid. I sometimes felt outnumbered, ganged-up on, unimportant, and not good enough. I struggled with the feeling that men were more important or better than women.

One night when I was about fifteen or sixteen years old, I sat in my bed crying and praying, saying, "I guess men are better than women. They hold the priesthood. They hold leadership positions in the Church and in the world. We don't read much of women in the scriptures."

Then, as clear as my own thoughts, I understood these words in my mind: "Jesus died for women too." I knew those words were from my Heavenly Father, that he sent them in answer to my prayer. I knew then in my heart that God regarded women as equal to men and that Jesus loved woman as he loved man.

I was able at that moment to dismiss all the untruths that I had almost accepted. I could go on with no doubt and for the rest of my life know that God loved me as much as he would have loved me if I were a man. I never again doubted Heavenly Father's regard for all his children. And while in some people's eyes women are the lesser of the two genders, I know and always will know that men and women are of equal value, worth, and importance in the eyes of God.

Arise and be baptized, and wash away your sins,
calling on my name, and you shall receive my Spirit,
and a blessing so great as you never have known.

D&C 39:10

"ARISE AND BE BAPTIZED"
AUTHOR UNKNOWN

For most of the thirty-nine years Samuel King [president of the Sudoeste District of the Uruguay-Paraguay Mission] spent as an administrator of a large meat-packing plant [in Montevideo, Uruguay], he was a staunch member of the Church of England. . . .

His first introduction to The Church of Jesus Christ of Latter-day Saints was on a bus carrying him and his wife and two children back to their home in Fray Bentos from Montevideo.

"When we reached the city of Rosario, a group of young men got on the bus and I noticed by their English that they were Americans. I eventually discovered they were player-missionaries of the Mormon Church, representing the Deseret basketball team.

"During the course of our journey, we exchanged names and conversation, and I extended to them an invitation to visit us when they reached Fray Bentos, which they did. At this time, I was quite unaware that there were missionaries of the Mormon

Church residing in Fray Bentos. I invited them to continue to visit us whenever they cared to, but on the condition that they would not try to convert my family, as I was not interested, and was a staunch member of the Church of England," he said.

The elders and their successors continued to call on the King family for four years after the first meeting.

Finally, Mrs. King asked her husband: "Why don't you let the boys tell you about their church? It can do you no harm, since you are so staunch in your own church."

President King explained, "I let them go ahead, and it was interesting to hear their views. That first night, I had the first discussion. I became more and more interested and at the end of four weeks, they gave me the story of Joseph Smith to read. At that time, I just could not bring myself to believe that Joseph Smith saw our Heavenly Father and the Lord Jesus Christ, or that he translated the Book of Mormon from gold plates given him by the angel Moroni.

"No matter how I tried, I just could not accept this; however, I did keep my promise to the elders and continued to read the Book of Mormon.

"I want to emphasize, however, that I had never read one word of the Doctrine and Covenants or the Pearl of Great Price. At this stage in my study, I came to the turning point of my life with a happening that was to convert me to the Church.

"It was on the night of October 19, 1966, that I had a dream. I want to emphasize again, that I had not read one word of the

Doctrine and Covenants, and was ignorant of what it was all about.

"In my dream, I saw the book of the Doctrine and Covenants open at section 39 and although I could read no words, I did see clearly the numbers 10 and 13. During the course of my dream, I reached out with my hand and closed the book five times, and on each occasion it opened again. On the sixth attempt to close it, it was not possible, as all physical strength seemed to have left me.

"With this I awoke with a start and found I was perspiring profusely—as if just having done some excessive exercise. I put on my beside light, which awoke my wife. She asked me what was wrong, and I told her of my dream, at the same time looking for section 39 in the Doctrine and Covenants," he explained.

He quoted verses 10 and 13 which read:

"But, behold, the days of thy deliverance are come, if thou wilt hearken to my voice, which saith unto thee: Arise and be baptized, and wash away your sins, calling on my name, and you shall receive my Spirit, and a blessing so great as you never have known. . . .

"Thou art called to labor in my vineyard, and to build up my church, and to bring forth Zion, that it may rejoice upon the hills and flourish."

He said that after reading the two verses, he realized that all his doubts had vanished, and that he should be baptized.

"I knew that what the missionaries had told me and the Joseph Smith story were true, and that the Book of Mormon was truly translated by the power of God.

"When the elders made their customary visit the next evening, I told them I was ready for baptism. They were skeptical until I told them of my dream.

"When I asked my wife how she felt about the Church, she smiled and said, 'I have believed it to be the true Church for some time, but have been waiting for you.'"

President King was baptized in the Uruguay River, October 22, 1966.

Slightly modified from "'Going Home' with Testimony of the Gospel," *Church News*, 22 May 1971, 11. Used by permission.

Whoso trusteth in the Lord, happy is he.

PROVERBS 16:20

"SUNSHINE IN MY SOUL"
GARRICK GREENHALGH

When the prophets said the gospel would go to the ends of the earth, they meant it. Guiuan, Samar, a small town in the Philippines, was further away from anywhere that I had ever been. I was approaching the last five months of my mission when I was told that I was transferring to Guiuan, a nine-hour trip by bus and jeep from the mission home. This area was generally known throughout the mission as "outer darkness" because it was so far away from anything. I came to learn that the name held true for a lot of things about Guiuan. I also learned some of the greatest lessons of my life while I was there.

My companion, Elder Macababad, and I tried to do our best to love the people in our area. We worked hard to bring the gospel to the people. Day after day we tracted and made street contacts, trying to find somebody who would listen to our message. We worked hard to serve the community so that the people might see we just wanted to help them; but they wouldn't even let us do that. As our efforts to bring the gospel to these people failed, we became somewhat depressed and negative towards the people. Then one day we visited Brother Lucio.

Brother Lucio had been a member for four years. He had accepted the gospel because an elder had given him rice when he had no food. He thought that a person who would give with no thought of reward must belong to the true church—so he was baptized. We knew that his favorite thing about the church was the hymns.

The first day we met him remains indelibly imprinted in my mind. His little shanty-house was made of cinder-blocks, which were so old they crumbled when you touched them. Pieces of scrap metal served as a roof. In many places the metal had rusted completely through, exposing him to torrential rains. An ill-fitting piece of plywood served as a door. Garbage and raw sewage ran down the gutter by his house. My heart felt sick, as it had a thousand times before, when I saw the abject poverty in which he lived. I wondered how anyone could live in such depressing circumstances.

Brother Lucio opened the door and graciously invited us in. It took a minute for my eyes to adjust to the darkness inside. As they did, I looked around to find a smoldering fire in one corner. A few dirty dishes lay in the ashes. The ceiling and walls were covered in soot, making the room look even gloomier. On the walls hung records with the names Frank Sinatra, Bing Crosby, and Glen Miller written on them. Soldiers from World War II had given them to him when they left the island. Their black color did little to brighten the room.

He invited us to sit on a bench and began talking to us about his life. He told us that when he joined the Church, his wife and children left him, his friends rejected him, and his community ostracized him. He said it was hard to be alone and that he got very lonely. The hymns, he said, were the only things that brought him comfort when he felt sad or alone. Elder Macababad and I stayed and talked for a while, then as we got ready to leave, we asked him if we could sing him a hymn. A broad smile covered his weathered face, exposing a toothless mouth. He stood slowly, walked to his table, shuffled through a stack of books, and picked out a well-used hymnal. I asked him to pick a song we could sing to him, so he started searching. But then he stopped suddenly and said *he* would sing to us his favorite song. Slowly, he turned the pages until he found the song. While gently smoothing the pages, he said to us, "Elders, when I am sad, I sing this song and I can't help but feel happy." He then began to sing these words:

> There is sunshine in my soul today,
> More glorious and bright
> Than glows in any earthly sky,
> For Jesus is my light. . . .
>
> There is gladness in my soul today,
> And hope and praise and love,
> For blessings which he gives me now,
> For joys laid up above.

Though he wasn't singing the right tune, and the tempo wasn't quite right, I had never heard anything so beautiful. With each verse he sang the words sunk deep into my soul, softening my heart and opening my mind beyond my own problems. Here was a little old man, who lived in darkness, with nothing in this world to comfort him—no family, no job, and no close friends— and yet he managed to see the light. A light beyond what this world had provided for him. He saw and felt the miracle of the light of Christ and His love. In it he found joy, comfort, and belonging. As he continued to sing, my eyes filled with tears of gratitude for all that I had. I felt ashamed for all the murmuring I had been doing. Suddenly, the burdens I carried were lightened. How small and insignificant were my temporary, passing discomforts compared to what this man lived through. I literally had everything but had failed to see it. Right then, I made up my mind to see the sunshine and let it into my soul. I determine that if Brother Lucio could see light in the midst of poverty, then I could see it in my life.

My testimony grew immeasurably from that experience and it has sustained me through every "trial" I have encountered since. Sometimes I'll forget what I learned and go on kicking against pricks (see Acts 9:5); but when I stop to think, my mind takes me back to a dark little shanty, literally at the ends of the earth, where I learned the joy of the gospel. And in my mind I can still hear Brother Lucio singing in his wavering voice, "There is sunshine in my soul today. . . ."

Inasmuch as you are diligent and humble,
and exercise the prayer of faith, behold, . . .
I shall send means unto you for your deliverance.

D&C 104:80

STUCK IN A STREAM
CINDEE KEISER

One spring my husband, Gene, and I decided to take our children up into some nearby mountains for a picnic. But what started as a beautiful day turned out to be something of a nightmare.

We got on a really muddy road, too muddy to turn around on without getting stuck, so when we came to a stream that crossed the road we decided to coax our old pickup over it. Then we really did get stuck. The more we tried to get out, the deeper the wheels went into the streambed. Finally it got dark, and we knew we were there for the night.

It was miserable. There we were with six children and three blankets crammed into the cab of an old pickup in freezing weather. Just when we thought things couldn't get worse, the water in the stream backed up, then backed up some more, until it entered the cab and formed a pool of ice water several inches deep on the floor. We had to hold our feet up to keep them from getting frozen.

Finally it was dawn, and Gene decided to take Tony, our oldest boy, and walk out to find help. They walked for hours, and didn't see a soul. As the time passed they became more and more discouraged; in the early afternoon they knelt and prayed for help. We had prayed before, but this time I guess the Lord knew that they had done all they could.

As soon as they stood from their prayer, Gene felt impressed to turn and go in a different direction. They had walked in that direction for less than fifteen minutes when a Jeep came over the hill. In the Jeep were two good priesthood holders who were wondering why they had had the feeling they should go in that direction, which was a detour from their original route.

It was three in the afternoon when Gene and Tony and our rescuers got back to us. And I don't need to tell you that we slept well that night. After a very thankful family prayer, of course.

And according to his faith there was a
mighty change wrought in his heart.

ALMA 5:12

I DIDN'T FEEL PEACE
AS A WIFE AND MOTHER
JODY HIGHAM PIERCE

From the day my first child was born I loved and treasured being a mother. I felt great joy in nurturing, teaching, and loving God's precious children, and I was grateful to be able to stay at home to care for my children.

When I was pregnant with my third child, however, I started to lose some of that joy of motherhood. I felt weighed down by tiredness, dirty dishes, and soiled laundry. I still loved my children greatly, but I felt like I couldn't handle the crying and the little quarrels very well.

Sometimes I felt trapped; because of my two small children, it was hard to go places and do the normal errands that need to be done in life. I often felt despair. It seemed like being a mother was too hard. Every day I prayed for hope.

I wanted more help from my husband. I often felt like I had to do everything myself—clean the house, get up with the kids at night, prepare all the food, do all the finances, and so forth. My husband and I would have recurring arguments about who didn't appreciate whom and who did more work than the other. If I asked him to help me, he would act annoyed or burdened—and if he did help, it was grudgingly.

I felt worn-out emotionally and physically. When my husband was around, I acted even more tired, hoping that he would see that I needed more help. But if I mentioned my tiredness, he would say, "I'm not feeling so good myself." I felt he was not listening to me or giving place to my feelings.

My children seemed to be fussier. I didn't feel peace in my home.

Finally I prayed and asked my Heavenly Father if there was something I could do to be happier. After my prayer, I felt that I should confide in my mother. I told her how I felt and then said, "I feel like my children need to have peace and I don't know how to accomplish it."

My mom asked, "Do your children not have peace because you don't have peace, or do you not have peace because your children don't have peace?"

I didn't know. I had never considered that the root of the problem might lie in me.

I went home and prayed some more, trying to be open to the idea that I was the one who needed to change. I didn't know what I could change. I didn't see anything that I was doing wrong. But I felt like I needed to be open.

Heavenly Father then started me on the amazing, challenging, eye-opening journey of changing my heart. He helped me to look at my life and myself with a true and honest view. He gently showed me that I had pride in dealing with my husband. I had anger and unforgiveness in my heart for many little things that my husband had done from the beginning and for not being exactly who I thought he should be.

This anger wasn't a to-the-surface, obvious anger that manifested itself in me wanting to yell a lot or to hit something. It was a deep, buried, subtle anger that manifested itself in little sarcastic remarks, in rolling my eyes behind my husband's back, or in feeling like I didn't want him to be around. Without my realizing it, it had become all-consuming. I had to be told about it by my Heavenly Father.

Because of my anger and unforgiving attitude, I was not allowing myself to love my husband as I needed to. I had been angry with him for so many little things that finally I was angry with him all the time. These feelings changed how I felt about our family and how I acted at home.

Learning these things took much prayer and caused much pain. I had to be humble enough to learn that I was doing something wrong after trying so hard for so many years to do everything right. Heavenly Father taught me the specific behaviors I was doing that were untrue to who I really was.

I could never have changed on my own. It was only through the atonement of Jesus Christ that I was able to be changed.

I asked Heavenly Father for a feeling of forgiveness, for a feeling of humility, for a feeling of deeper, truer love, and he gave them to me because of my submissiveness, repentant heart, and willingness to be changed.

It was a process. I had to practice and evaluate and pray some more. I still have to be conscious of my feelings and actions and be totally forgiving and humble or I will slip back.

The result of this change was greater than I ever would have imagined. It affected my whole life and my everyday feelings about life. I was not as tired, the despair was lifted, the arguments disappeared.

I still felt that I needed more help from my husband, but with the right feeling I was able to gently encourage him to help or let it go. I stopped my untrue behaviors. I started to be free to feel the joy of motherhood and not focus on the burdens of being a mother.

As a result of these things, our home was given the spirit of peace. Our marriage has been getting better and better. A lot of things in marriage are still hard, but how I *feel* has changed. My husband feels more appreciated and loved, and in turn treats the children and me with more love. He is happier at home. I feel lighter and truer. I feel great joy in the moments I spend with my children and in serving them.

Now I have four children and my days are filled with minds to teach, spirits to influence, hugs from little arms, children in my arms or on my lap, and being surrounded by some of my favorite people. My days are also filled with the great burdens of motherhood, but Heavenly Father has given me the gift of peace and joy that helps me look past the burdens to see the greatness of being a wife and mother. This has been one of the greatest miracles of my life.

Then he took the five loaves and the two fishes,
and . . . blessed them, and brake, and gave
to the disciples to set before the multitude.
And they did eat, and were all filled.

LUKE 9:16–17

TWO BAGS OF CEMENT
JOHN PURSER

In June 1964, we were pouring the concrete floors in the chapel and recreational hall of the Poverty Bay District and Gisborne [New Zealand] Second Branch Chapel. There had been storms in the area for three weeks and the boats had not been able to deliver cement to Gisborne. We had borrowed all the cement there was within eighty miles, and when we quit work for lunch on the last day of pouring, we had just two bags of cement left and needed two and a half yards of concrete—enough to fill an area fifteen feet by thirteen feet. This would have required twelve bags of concrete to complete the job. As we returned from lunch everyone was saying, "We may as well not even start again; it wouldn't even be worthwhile."

I told them to start the mixer; that we were not only going to pour, but we would complete our floors that day. Then, not knowing at the time how it could be done, I walked a short distance from the group and prayed. I simply said, "Father, you fed the thousands with the five loaves and two fishes. Surely you can help us this day."

We went to work and mixed two small one-fourth yard batches of concrete with the two bags of cement we had and started pouring. There seemed to be no end to the concrete as it poured from our wheelbarrows. The full pour was not only completed, but we had to remove two wheelbarrows full when it was leveled out.

There is no physical way this could have been done by men. It was indeed a modern miracle performed for his people of the latter days.

Purser, in *The Builders Testify*, 3.

Be thou humble; and the Lord thy God shall lead thee by the hand,
and give thee answer to thy prayers.

D&C 112:10

"HAVE YOU CONSIDERED EVERYONE?"
R. REED CHANNELL

When I learned that my first counselor was moving, I considered each of the fine men in our ward as a possible replacement. I had set Saturday as my deadline in finding a man to recommend. On Thursday I made a list of twenty men whom I felt were worthy and compatible to the call. By Saturday morning the list had been cut to three. As I looked at these three names, one seemed best qualified. I reached for the phone to inform the stake president of my recommendation. Suddenly, a very strong impression came, and I said to myself, "Have you considered everyone?" I picked up my bishop's book and began to go through the list of members again. Halfway through I chuckled at myself, feeling certain the right choice had already been made. But obedient to my impression I continued through the book until my finger fell on a certain name. It is difficult to describe the feeling that came to me. It was as if a dynamic spiritual force rang through my whole body, testifying of my counselor.

Tears streamed from my eyes in thankfulness to the Lord for

this revelation. The man was not the one I had formerly selected. He was not among my final three. He was not even among the twenty. He was a man with whom I had experienced little contact, and because my knowledge of him was so limited, I had not considered him. When I was called to participate in his ordination, I worried that I had made a mistake or been deceived in my selection; but the Lord, sensing my weakness, presented me an exact duplication of my previous experience. I have since thought how important the call of counselor must be for the Lord to reveal his will in such a manner. But, more than anything, the experience taught me that one must rely on the Lord and not on his own judgment.

"How I Was Guided in Selecting a Counselor," *Improvement Era*, September 1966, 822.

Cast thy burden upon the Lord, and he shall sustain thee.

PSALM 55:22

"MY BURDEN IS LIGHT"
DAVID C. HOLBROOK

My brother was called to be a bishop a year or two after I was. I asked him early on how he was doing in his calling. His answer: "I have never seen so many sad people in my life."

I reflected on how true that is. A bishop works with many wonderful people; he sees impressive demonstrations of faith and devotion and sacrifice for the Lord and for the Church. He works with members who will do anything they are asked. On occasion he has the great privilege of having a member share a precious spiritual experience with him. He sees the hard work of various members of the ward, who give their all and then more—Relief Society presidents, Scoutmasters, nursery leaders, stake missionaries, some home and visiting teachers.

But members don't often come to a bishop to tell him what's going right in their lives. Those who most commonly seek out a bishop are those who are having troubles. Those with marital problems, wayward children, sins that must be confessed, persistent welfare needs, nagging habits that keep them from the temple—a bishop sees all these and more.

As I began my service I was counseled by a friend at work (who was a stake president in another part of the city) not to bear the members' burdens myself.

I thought much about that counsel. I knew that our Savior has issued a powerful invitation to us all: "Come unto me, all ye that labour and are heavy laden, and I will give you rest. Take my yoke upon you, and learn of me; for I am meek and lowly in heart: and ye shall find rest unto your souls. For my yoke is easy, and my burden is light" (Matthew 11:28–30). And I read in the Psalms, "Cast thy burden upon the Lord, and he shall sustain thee: he shall never suffer the righteous to be moved" (Psalm 55:22).

More than once I went home from a long Sunday weighed and burdened by the troubles and problems of the members of my ward. They would confide in me about abusive relationships, or marriages that had grown cold, or parents who didn't seem to understand, or commandments that were being broken, and I would *feel* the burden of it. Sometimes I would carry the weight on my shoulders for days. Sometimes I would receive a particularly heavy weight on Sunday, carry it through the week, and then pick up a new one the following Sunday.

I don't want to suggest that there weren't plenty of opportunities to rejoice with members for the gifts and blessings the Lord was pouring out on their heads. If he is in tune with the Spirit, a bishop can receive blessings in his relationships with members that far exceed the cost of any time or effort he expends.

But still I carried that weight.

Not many weeks went by, however, when I realized it was

time for me to repent. The Lord knows how to succor those who are burdened (Alma 7:12)—and I was not partaking of that which he offered me. I was trying to be a servant without partaking of the resources offered by the Master.

That night, before I went home from the bishop's office, I knelt alone and talked it out with the Lord. I told him that I knew of his promises, and I expressed sorrow that I had been carrying the burdens of many ward members by myself. I asked him to forgive me. And then I asked him to take from me the burdens I had been carrying. I knew it was possible by the power of the Atonement, and I now sought to claim those blessings for myself.

As I prayed the Spirit rested on me and filled me with peace. I could feel a literal lightening of the load on my shoulders. I felt my heart and mind clear. When I finally stood on my feet and proceeded home, I did so with deep gratitude and rejoicing.

In the remaining years of my service, I followed the same practice repeatedly whenever I helped a ward member with a difficult situation. I taught them that they could share the burden with the Lord. And then, when I was alone, I reminded myself that I must do the same. I knelt and offered the burden to him—and every time he took it.

Whosoever shall call on the name of the Lord shall be delivered.

—JOEL 2:32

LEAVE FOR WEST BERLIN TODAY
DIETER BERNDT

In 1960, I was living near Hamburg in West Germany and was called to be the mission YMMIA president. Half of the members of our mission lived in East Germany, which necessitated having counterpart Young Men's and Young Ladies' presidents serving in the same capacity in East Germany. Because the Church members were scattered over a large area, we made a special effort to plan as many activities as possible that could be attended by all the youth of the mission. This presented some problems peculiar to our mission, since half the mission was in West Germany and West Berlin, and the other half was behind the Iron Curtain. It was impossible to hold any activities in the eastern sector, so we scheduled all of our programs in West Berlin so that the East Germans could also attend. They could easily board a subway in East Berlin, ride across the border into West Berlin and attend the meeting, then return to their homes without difficulty.

Shortly after I was called to this position, we began planning for our most important and largest activity of the year, which was to be a youth conference to be held in West Berlin during the Easter holiday. I began corresponding with the Young Men's and Young Women's presidents in East Germany and managed to complete all the arrangements for the conference by mail.

The conference was a tremendous success—very inspiring and very enjoyable. For me, the most interesting part on the program was a musical number by a very attractive and talented young lady—the Young Women's president from East Germany with whom I had been corresponding.

I immediately took advantage of the first opportunity to become acquainted with Gisaliela and was even more impressed with her as I got to know her. During the months that followed, our correspondence continued, and before long we began meeting in West Berlin whenever possible. We began to make plans for our future together and made the necessary unauthorized arrangements for her to come to Hamburg to meet my family during her vacation. Gisaliela's mother was to accompany her to East Berlin on Tuesday, August 15, where they would spend the night with her brother before continuing on to West Berlin to pick up their airline tickets for Hamburg.

The Sunday morning before Gisaliela was due to arrive, Mother and I attended church services in Hamburg as usual, but the priesthood meeting did not proceed as usual—it was announced that the Berlin Wall had been put up during the night and *all* traffic between East and West Berlin had been terminated! I was heartsick. The girl I wanted to marry was in East Germany and she would not be permitted to leave. This meant that we could not be married as we had planned.

I was so upset by this news that I decided that I would leave immediately for West Berlin to see if there was something that I could do to make arrangements for Gisaliela to leave East Germany. Knowing full well the futility of trying to deal with the Communist-controlled government, Mother told me that there was no point in my going to Berlin, for she was sure that there was nothing I could do.

I was very discouraged and dejected that Sunday morning as Mother and I knelt in prayer and asked the Lord for his help. We hoped, and prayed fervently, that somehow the Lord would help us so that Gisaliela and I could be reunited.

I was so disheartened that I couldn't concentrate on what any of the speakers had to say or on the lessons. I returned home and found that a telegram from Gisaliela was waiting for me. I couldn't believe it—she was in *West* Berlin! It was unbelievable, incomprehensible! She was not due in West Berlin for several more days!

The following Friday Gisaliela arrived at the Hamburg airport. She then told me the following story of how she came to be in West Berlin on that Saturday afternoon a few hours before the Berlin Wall went up:

"Saturday morning I was busy preparing for a district meeting when my father came into the room and said, 'I want you to leave for West Berlin today.' I replied that Mother and I had made all the arrangements to leave on Tuesday, and besides, I had to prepare for the district meeting, but my father insisted that we leave for West Berlin immediately! When I asked for a reason why we should leave early, his only reply was that he didn't know why—he just *knew* that we should leave as soon as possible.

"I couldn't understand this—it was so unlike my father to irrationally and illogically make this type of decision. I asked him again for a good reason and he said, 'I can't give you a good reason. I just have this uneasy feeling and I feel impressed that you should leave now for West Berlin.' He refused to discuss the matter further and told my mother that she was to leave with me and cautioned us not to make any stops along the way.

"He was so determined that Mother and I decided to do as he asked. We packed our bags and were on the next train to Berlin. We found out later that this was the last train we could have taken to Berlin. There were no more tickets sold after that train departed.

"We had previously planned to spend our first evening in East Berlin with my brother and in a day or two cross over into West Berlin and pick up our airline tickets at a friend's home. For some reason, we decided to continue on to the friend's house to pick up the tickets, with the intention of returning to East Berlin that evening and spending the night. However, when we picked up the tickets our friend suggested that we spend the night, so, quite contrary to our plans, we accepted the invitation and spent the night in West Berlin.

"You can imagine the shock we experienced when we awoke the next morning and found that the Berlin Wall had gone up during the night and the border had been closed. Even now, it's hard to comprehend that such a thing could actually happen. I'm so very grateful that my Heavenly Father inspired my earthly father to have me leave the day before the wall was constructed. I'm also thankful that I was obedient and listened to his inspired advice.

"Mother, of course, wanted to be with my father, who was the branch president, so she returned to East Germany that morning. We parted with heavy hearts, not knowing when, or if ever we would see each other again."

When Gisaliela related her experience to me, I knew that the Lord had opened the way for us to be married and that our marriage would be very special, and it has been.

The Lord has truly blessed us and allowed us to be brought together by forces that cannot be explained by human powers. The power of the Holy Ghost to guide and inspire each of us is real. Gisaliela and I can bear witness that this is so, for our lives have been altered dramatically by obeying the promptings of the still small voice. A miracle was truly performed in our behalf.

Jensen, *Stories of Insight and Inspiration*, 115–18.

I know in whom I have trusted. My God hath been my support;
he hath led me through mine afflictions in the wilderness;
and he hath preserved me upon the waters of the great deep.

2 NEPHI 4:19–20

HE WRAPPED HER LEGS IN HOT TOWELS
DEE ANN BARROWES

In the years just before the polio vaccine was introduced, my mother contracted a severe case of polio. The best care for those with polio was debatable. The general practice was to hospitalize the patient, and some required the use of an "iron lung," which helped them to breathe as their chest muscles became weaker and eventually were paralyzed. Some never recovered. This heart-breaking disease was known to cripple, paralyze, and even kill its helpless victims.

Unfortunately, my family did not have much money for the care of Mother. We had no health insurance, and hospital care was, even then, very expensive. My father wrestled with the dilemma. He wanted the best possible care for my mother, and yet he had no way to pay for it.

Finally, he made the very difficult decision that he would keep his wife at home and give her the best care he could. He prayed mightily to the Lord that he would sustain and help him in his decision, and he felt a certain amount of peace about it. He pleaded that his choice would not cause further harm to my mother or increase the ill effects of the disease.

My father gave many, many hours and days and months of tender care. He would frequently heat towels in hot water on the stove and wrap mother's legs. Some health-care providers may have disagreed with his approach, but he felt it was the right thing for him to do. Mother's case was severe enough that she remained bedridden for many months.

Even as a very young girl I felt the responsibility to help. I did all I could, especially when my father was away at work. I remember his red hands when he handled the hot towels. I did not do as well with the towels as he did.

Eventually and gradually, my mother began to improve. We all watched, hoping that our prayers would be answered, that she would be able to be all right. When the doctors saw her, they were amazed at the completeness of her recovery. She had little evidence of the devastating sickness. She was able to function normally and had very few lasting effects.

Our family knew what power had caused her healing and were grateful beyond measure for the answer to our prayers.

These words are not of men nor of man, but of me; . . . and by my
power you can read them one to another; . . . wherefore, you can
testify that you have heard my voice, and know my words.

D&C 18:34–36

THE SPIRIT TEACHES SCRIPTURE
JEAN ASAY

Our daughter was just beginning her sophomore year in high school. With all the excitement surrounding the first school dance of the year and with many of her friends going with dates, she became painfully aware of how long it would be before her sixteenth birthday—May 25. Her awareness was heightened when she, too, was invited to go to the first dance. She replied, with commitment, that she was waiting until she turned sixteen to date. But, she admitted later, it did seem like a challenge to miss all of the dances and date activities for the year ahead of her.

Two months later she was invited to attend another school dance, which had a number of daytime activities associated with it. Many of her friends were going, the appeal became more than she had anticipated, and finally she asked if she could accept this one date. She assured us that she did not intend to make it a regular thing, but wondered if this one time couldn't be an exception. The more she talked about it, the more she wanted to go, until finally, after a week of hoping that her desire would pass, we realized we needed to help her make the right decision and feel good about it—instead of our just saying no.

After much prayer and thought and sensing her deep feelings, we pondered the situation together one evening. I felt a little uncertain as I heard myself finally saying to her, "If you will take one week to study your scriptures with this question in your heart, and pray about it in a way that you can hear Heavenly Father's answer—not just your own desire, but Heavenly Father's answer—we will abide by your decision." I was somewhat surprised that I had put us in that situation, but I had felt impressed to say it. She assured me that she would do her best.

Less than a week later she came to us saying that she had made her decision. She said she had received an answer—but it was not the one she wanted. She had done as we had asked, and one night while she was reading, a passage of scripture was transferred off the page and into her heart by the Spirit. She knew not only that it was true but also that it had personal relevance for her at this particular time:

"Verily I say, men should be anxiously engaged in a good cause, and do many things of their own free will, and bring to pass much righteousness;

"For the power is in them, wherein they are agents unto themselves. And inasmuch as men do good they shall in nowise lose their reward.

"But he that doeth not anything until he is commanded, and

receiveth a commandment with doubtful heart, and keepeth it with slothfulness, the same is damned" (D&C 58:27–29).

The course, which had seemed so vague to her before, was now clear. She had no doubt. She was content.

In a moment of her life when I had the courage to step back and let scripture and Spirit blend their power in instruction, our daughter learned more profoundly than she ever could have from my feeble reasoning.

Ayres, *Great Teaching Moments*, 1–2.

Counsel with the Lord in all thy doings,
and he will direct thee for good.

ALMA 37:37

HE FOUND US ON THE MAP
EVA DAWN JONES

One of the hardest challenges in my family of many children has been that most of them have suffered from dyslexia, a learning disability. Each of them, to a greater or a lesser degree, has struggled with schoolwork and, even though they have each handled the challenges in acceptable ways, it certainly has not been easy.

The youngest daughter in our family exhibited the symptoms of dyslexia early, and it seemed severe. She had a terrible time in first grade. She was miserable as she tried to understand why a lot of the schoolwork didn't make sense to her and why she couldn't seem to learn the alphabet.

When we built our home on the edge of an established neighborhood, we were informed that we were in the boundaries for Wilson Elementary School. This school was not the closest to us, but it was the one where all of the neighbor children attended and so that is where we sent our children. (The closer elementary school was Adams Elementary School.)

As parents, we struggled mightily to understand how to help this unhappy and stressed child. We made it a matter of a lot of prayer and fasting, wishing for Heavenly Father's help, knowing that she was his child as well.

During the summer, my husband and I decided to attend BYU Education Week. We were enjoying the time away and were not particularly thinking about the challenges at home. I was attending a class that had nothing to do with parenting or educational challenges when the following sentence came into my mind: "Send your daughter to Adams Elementary and have her do first grade again."

This was a surprising understanding. We had never considered Adams Elementary, since we didn't live in its boundaries. And I was hesitant to have her repeat a grade when she disliked school so much.

I wondered if it was truly an inspiration. I prayed and asked Heavenly Father if these words had come from him. The answer was "yes."

My husband and I had agreed to meet at the car for a lunch break. As we got into the car to eat, I shared with my husband the words that had come into my mind. I asked if he would pray to see if the understanding was from Heavenly Father. We both prayed hard. The answer was very plain. We were to send our daughter to Adams Elementary and have her repeat first grade.

Within the next few days I made an appointment at the new school and asked that my daughter be enrolled in first grade there. I was informed that the enrollment of the school was very high and the classes were crowded. They were not accepting any new students who did not live within the school boundaries—no exceptions. I was very disappointed and wondered why we had been impressed to make the request.

I went home and told my husband about my experience. He decided to go to the school himself. As he was waiting in the school hallway for the principal, he noticed a map on the wall. Being a map buff, he went over and noticed that it was a map of the school boundaries. He looked very carefully, trying to locate our home on the map. When he found it he saw that the boundary line ran between our house and all of the other houses in the neighborhood, right along our yard. Our home was the only house in the neighborhood that was actually within the boundary lines of Adams Elementary.

When the principal came out of his office, they looked at the map together; then the principal said, "Well, I guess there is nothing I can say. Your daughter will certainly be welcome here."

Our daughter repeated first grade at Adams Elementary School. She had a wonderful teacher. She had good friends and began to learn how to compensate for and overcome her learning disability.

With very hard work and a lot of determination, she graduated from high school with excellent grades; she was even invited to join the scholastic honor society. She received many awards and acknowledgments, and we are proud of her. And we are so thankful for a loving Father who gave us the inspiration we needed for one of his children.

GOD GIVE ME STRENGTH!
Blaine Rasmussen

We had driven to Butterfield Canyon for a picnic, and as our then family of five children were excitedly leaving the car, one of the children alighted from the right side of the car and, assuming that his brothers and sisters had exited from the other door, slammed the door with a firmness that would guarantee that he would not have to return and repeat the action.

Agonizing screams coming from the back seat made us immediately aware that his assumption was not correct. I bolted from the driver's seat to the source of the outcry to find that Byron's hand had been trapped between the door and the door post.

I immediately pulled back on the car door to open it, but it did not budge. Again, using all my strength, which I am sure under the stress of seeing my own child in agony and pain must have exceeded my normal strength, I struggled desperately to open that door. But the door did not open. It was as if it had been welded shut.

Panic seized me as thoughts raced through my mind as to the

amount of time it would take for me to retrieve the keys from inside the car, walk to the trunk, open it, obtain a tire-bar, return to the door, pry it open, and the damage that would occur to my child's hand during the few minutes it would take for this process—too much time!

I needed help—the kind of help only my Heavenly Father could give. I again took a firm grasp on the door handle, braced myself and pleaded, *"God, give me strength!"*

Then, once more I attempted to open the door, and did so seemingly without effort. It was as if the door almost exploded open, as it opened so fast that I fell backwards, taking a couple of steps before I could regain my equilibrium.

As the car door opened, my child's hand was released, the hand and fingers very flat and completely without feeling.

Upon examination, we found that the skin had not even been broken, nor did it appear as if the bones were broken. Within the hour, the fingers had resumed their usual shape— plump and rounded, the sensation of feeling returned, and, all in all, the hand was normal.

The power and strength of the Lord was there when I needed it. All I had to do was ask, and it was given.

Jensen, *When Faith Writes the Story*, 63–64.

I have made, and I will bear; even I will carry, and will deliver you.

ISAIAH 46:4

THE LORD HAD PROMISED HIS HELP
R. SAMUEL RIRIE

Before we had our youngest child, who is now nearly ten, we went to the Lord to make sure we were doing his will to have another baby. We had six children already. I was quite concerned about the age and health of my wife, Janet. Her health was fine, but she was nearing the end of her childbearing years, and we didn't want to take any chances. We were also concerned about finances, because we had no health insurance at the time.

As we prayed repeatedly about what to do, the Spirit reassured us all would be well with Janet physically, and that the Lord would take care of us financially.

But as time for the birth approached, we learned that our baby was in the breech position, which would make a normal delivery impossible for Janet, who was small to begin with. The doctor warned us that he might well have to perform a C-section. We worried anew about health issues and the greatly increased costs if Janet had surgery. Since the Lord had promised us help, we went to him in confidence, fasting and praying that our baby would turn and change positions. We felt that the Lord was near and that he would take care of our every need. But the baby never did turn. The doctor scheduled a C-section and delivered us a fine baby daughter according to schedule.

We rejoiced when Janet recovered quickly. And the baby's health was fine. But now we had that terrible hospital bill and only moderate income. What had happened to our prayers? Why hadn't the baby turned when we asked the Lord? And why were we left with those huge hospital and doctor bills when the Lord had told us less than a year earlier that he would take care of us? Our faith wavered, but we continued to pray.

Then the Lord began to provide money so that we could start to pay off our debt. I was able to get some extra work that brought in additional income for a time. Little by little for the next few months we made payments on the hospital bill. But the hospital was getting impatient. Then one day we got a statement from the hospital thanking us for paying the bill in full. We were shocked and amazed. I went to the hospital to clear things up, because we still owed several thousand dollars. I looked over the bill with one of their accountants. It had indeed been fully paid, with one large payment at the end to pay it off.

Janet and I had no idea who our secret benefactor was. But of course we knew who really had paid the bill: The Lord had paid it, using as his instruments someone who loved him and loved us.

Our fervent prayers that all would be well with the pregnancy both physically and financially were not answered in the way we expected. But we can never deny that the Lord did indeed answer our prayers, blessing us abundantly.

Whatsoever ye ask the Father in my name it shall be given unto you, that is expedient for you.

I WAS UNABLE TO READ EVEN ONE NAME
JOAN LLOYD HOFHEINS

My mother's family, the Edward Ashton family, has always been mindful of their obligation to seek out the records of our departed kindred. My early adult years had been filled with the time-consuming demands of raising a large family of my own, so it was not until the last few years that I started to assume my share of the responsibility for doing our family genealogy.

I was given the assignment of reading the microfilms of a parish register from Wales that was recorded in the early 1600s. The original register was written in Old English script and Latin, which is difficult to read in a perfectly preserved record. This particular register, however, was in exceptionally poor condition, with many of the pages being well worn and parts of the record so blurred as to make it almost illegible.

My aunt had told me that we had about ten to twelve family lines that had been recorded in this particular parish register. She

stated that I would find the names of a great many of our ancestors on those rolls of film, which were so numerous that it would
take a year or more to read all of them. I was instructed that every
name that was one of our family surnames would be a relative,
and when we had recorded their genealogical information, the
temple work could be done for these people, thereby bringing the
blessings of the gospel ordinances to a great number of our
departed kindred.

I greatly felt my responsibility to those that had gone before
me, but the task of completing this time-consuming record and
also meeting the daily needs of my family seemed to be almost
impossible, though I had the assurance that I would be able to do
the work for these ancestors if I were prayerful and had the Spirit
of the Lord with me. Thus, it was with a great measure of enthu-
siasm and confidence that I went to the reading room at the BYU
library and proceeded to put the microfilm on the reading
machine. I adjusted the machine to bring the film into sharp
focus and was shocked to find that the film was not one bit more
readable when it was in focus than when it was out of focus. The
Old English script looked like a foreign language to me and could
not have been more difficult for me to decipher had it actually
been a foreign language. I was overwhelmed with the impossi-
bility of my being able to read that record, and quickly came to
the conclusion that I was either going to have to have special
training in reading English script and Latin, or I would have to
get someone else to read the film for me.

I sat for a few moments, disappointed and dejected at having failed to accomplish my assignment. I had not been able to read even one name on the film. And then, as I sat and contemplated what my purpose was in trying to read the film, I realized that I had given up very quickly, without having done everything I possibly could to read the record. There was one thing more I could do, and that was to pray. So I bowed my head and said a short prayer and asked the Lord to please help me to understand the Old English script and to be able to read the names of my ancestors that were recorded on that roll of film.

I then decided to try to read the film once more. The first page of the register was so poorly preserved that I felt that it would be impossible to ever read any of the names on that page, even if I mastered the art of reading Old English script. I decided that I would turn the film forward to another page that was more legible when I received the distinct impression that some of the people listed on that page had been waiting longer to have their temple work done than those whose names would appear in more recent and readable records. I also received a very strong impression that they were just as important as anyone else whose name would appear later in those records, and needed their work done as much as did the others, if not more.

As I continued to look at the strange penmanship on that page, a miracle began to take place! Certain names gradually became very clear and I could easily read them and determine that they were my ancestors. I read on and was able to decipher the dates of birth, baptism, and deaths of those who had our family surnames. After I recorded this information and turned the viewer to the next page of the register, *all* of the handwriting would be illegible. After looking at the page intently for a few moments, another name would suddenly start to clear and I was able to easily read the information on that family member while all the writing surrounding it was totally unreadable. It was a thrilling experience for me as I gratefully recorded many names of my ancestors that day.

I excitedly related the experience to my family that evening, and they were also impressed with the way the Lord had helped me to read the microfilm. My sixteen-year-old daughter Carolyn was especially impressed and touched by this experience and requested that she be given the opportunity to try to read the film. I was delighted at her interest, but felt that I should caution her that it would take more than just a casual interest and curiosity to be able to read the record. I told her that she would have to prepare herself spiritually first, by fasting and prayer. This she willingly did, and excitedly joined me at the library, hoping and praying that she would also be given the blessing of being able to read the record.

It was a very choice and exciting experience for both of us as Carolyn had exactly the same experience of having the Spirit of the Lord help her to read the names of our ancestors. We could feel that guiding influence of the Spirit as we continued to "read" through the films that day. Several times we were prompted to recheck a certain area of the film, only to find that we had missed a name. In our excitement to progress as fast as possible with the work, we had turned the film ahead without waiting sufficiently for the Spirit to assist us in reading the film. This was truly a testimony to me that those people were ready and waiting to have their work done in the temples of the Lord and were there to assist in completing their record.

My fifteen-year-old son Timothy, who has also received a testimony of the work for the redemption of the dead, requested the privilege of assisting with the reading of the microfilms. After a period of fasting and prayer, he too joined us at the library and had the same experiences as we had had in reading the films. The three of us have since spent many enjoyable and rewarding hours reading the films of that parish register and have been able to record the names and dates of more than four hundred of our ancestors.

It has been a very thrilling and gratifying experience for me to share in my children's love for their departed kindred, even to the point where they have encouraged and prodded me in the work of completing our family genealogy. And this experience has also been an unforgettable witness to me that the Lord loves *all* his children and ministers to their needs, even those who are "dead."

Jensen, *Stories of Insight and Inspiration*, 89–92.

I did pour out my whole soul unto God.

ENOS 1:9

THE LORD WAS READY
CHRISTIE ANN GILES

As I knelt by my bed to say my nightly prayers, I felt like my heart would burst—not with joy, but with loneliness and anger. This wasn't what I had expected at all!

It was my second night at the Missionary Training Center in Provo, Utah, and I was feeling miserable. I didn't like my companion, I didn't like Spanish, and I didn't like myself much for being such a baby.

I started my prayer, but then realized that I didn't have anything to say. Although I desperately needed someone to talk to, it just didn't seem right to express my empty, lonely, and bitter feelings to Heavenly Father. I finally said a standard, "thank you for my health and the chance to be here," sort of prayer and crawled into bed.

Why doesn't Heavenly Father help me? If he really knows how I feel before I ask, what is he waiting for? I thought angrily.

Then I remembered the book of Enos, which I had read that afternoon. I pictured Enos kneeling in the forest, pleading for the

Lord to forgive and help him. His words echoed in my mind: "I did pour out my whole soul unto God" (Enos 1:9).

Had I done the same? Had I really humbly asked for Heavenly Father's help? I knew I hadn't.

I knelt again. This time I had plenty to say. I told my Father how frustrated I felt, how I couldn't learn the language, how I needed to love my companion, and how I wanted to do a good job. I cried as I explained that I felt abandoned, and I needed his help.

"And ye shall seek me, and find me, when ye shall search for me with all your heart" (Jeremiah 29:13).

This time I didn't say a prayer—I prayed. Again, I felt that my heart would burst, but this time with hope, peace, and love. As I climbed into bed, I still didn't know how things would work out, but I knew they would.

"A Change of Heart." Christie Ann Giles. Previously published in *The New Era*, November 1991, 11. © by Intellectual Reserve, Inc. Used by permission.

O Lord, wilt thou grant unto us that we may have success
in bringing them again unto thee in Christ.
Behold, O Lord, their souls are precious.

ALMA 31:34–35

. . . UNTIL THEY KNOW WE CARE
ROBERT L. MILLET

My first experience with teaching seminary began with five classes of ninth graders. I entered the classroom with great expectations, to say the least. I had enjoyed teaching the gospel to nonmembers while on a mission, had taught the Gospel Doctrine class in Sunday School for a number of years, and felt that to be involved in a weekday religious education program would be the highlight of my life. In my loftiest moments I had anticipated walking into the room, inviting the Spirit of the Lord to be with us through prayer, and "holding hands with God" for an hour while I witnessed the Holy Spirit working wondrous changes in the lives of a group of eager and theologically thirsty young people.

Somehow reality took a different turn. I found a surprising number in each class to be disrespectful, rude, insensitive, and almost totally uninterested in the marvelous things I had prepared to share with them. They chattered and laughed and occupied themselves irreverently with other things all through the class. This went on day after day.

One afternoon during fifth period one of my more challenging young men came into class late; the lesson had started some ten or fifteen minutes earlier. He walked up to me with his hands behind his back, and, while grinning broadly, said, "Brother Millet, I brought you something."

I said, "OK, Bill, what is it?"

At that point he retrieved from behind his back a can of plastic foam. He covered me with the stuff—my face, my hair, my new suit of clothes. I can still recall the first thought I had at that moment: I don't remember Elder Packer's book, *Teach Ye Diligently*, dealing with a problem quite like this one.

I "quit my job" every afternoon for three months. My wife, Shauna, would buoy me up with, "Come on, now, you can do it. You have something to offer. Be patient with them."

My principal was understanding and sensitive to my soul-struggling. He listened each day at lunch and empathized with my dilemma. He was also quite a humorist. I remember his saying to me, "Bob, do you know what my behavioral objective was for today? It was to leave the classroom at the end of the day of my own free will and while standing on my own two feet." Although his understanding and ready laughs did much to assure me that others were likewise struggling, the pain known only to those who have a vital message but few listening ears pierced my heart regularly.

My prayers during those early fall months were pointed and

direct. There was no beating around the bush here: "O God, please change these wayward youth. Please help them to appreciate me and my message. Please open their eyes that they may see." Such prayers were neither vain nor shallow; I was pleading from the depths of my soul. I meant what I said. My desires were not unrighteous; I wanted my students to come to love the scriptures and love the Lord as I did. Well, God is merciful and he does answer prayers. And so it was that eyes were opened.

It was during one of my prayers at night—a prayer in behalf of my classes—that the stirrings of change began: stirrings within my own heart. On that glorious day I learned a lesson that would serve me for life. Having expressed what I had planned to say, I allowed some additional time on my knees for pondering and reflection. After a few moments there came a desire for further prayer. My words reached beyond my thoughts and I began to learn much from what was said; prayer became more than petitionary—it became instructive. My thoughts turned to the young people I taught; my own feelings were swallowed up in a love for them which I had never known. I felt a great need to repent of self-centeredness and an overwhelming desire to express my love for my students. My prayers changed. My petitions were now such things as, "O Lord, help me to be worthy of these great souls, for I know that they are precious in thy sight."

I didn't sleep much for the rest of the night. Morning finally came, and as I knelt in prayer beside my bed in the early hours of the day I pleaded one more time with the Lord—but this time I asked that the feelings of the night before might be manifest in my teaching that day. As I looked over the class in first period my heart and soul went out to them in love, as though there had been an opening of the windows of heaven. I told them how much I loved them. I told them what a privilege it was to teach them. I asked their forgiveness for my impatience and my spiritual short-sightedness. As I looked into their eyes I saw similar feelings in them and knew that we had communicated. More especially, we had been edified and were rejoicing together. Discipline problems were few thereafter. Relationships blossomed during the rest of the year and lasting friendships were forged which I hope to renew again and again in this life and into the next.

Some years later I was studying the Book of Mormon when I discovered an incident which took on new meaning for me. After Alma and his missionary companions had discovered the doctrinally deplorable condition of the Zoramites, and just prior to their ministry among these apostates, Alma prayed in disgust, "O, how long, O Lord, wilt thou suffer that thy servants shall dwell here below in the flesh, to behold such gross wickedness among the children of men? . . . O Lord God, how long wilt thou suffer that such wickedness and infidelity shall be among this people? O Lord, wilt thou give me strength, that I may bear with mine infirmities . . . O Lord, my heart is exceedingly sorrowful; . . . wilt thou comfort my soul, and give unto me success, and also my fellow laborers who are with me."

Alma's prayer continued. Perhaps the Spirit of the Lord began to mold and shape and focus Alma's prayer further; his heart began to turn toward the Zoramites, not in revulsion but in reverence; not with bitterness but with benevolence. And thus Alma finally prayed, "O Lord, wilt thou grant unto us that we may have success in bringing them again unto thee in Christ. Behold, O Lord, their souls are precious" (Alma 31:26–35).

Surely the message of the gospel—the message of peace and love—is communicated more effectively and incorporated more lastingly when the teacher is a vessel of love, when he or she has come to view from God's perspective those to whom the message is to be delivered. How truly appropriate is the aphorism, "People don't care how much we know until they know how much we care."

Ayres, *Great Teaching Moments*, 11–14.

After much tribulation come the blessings.

D&C 58:4

I APPLIED ON THE LAST DAY
John J. McIntyre

When I lost my job in August of 1998 at age fifty-three, I became very discouraged. I tried for months to find another job, but to no avail. Our condition became desperate. Not only did we lose my income, but we also lost our health insurance. My health had been poor for several years. I had had prostate cancer not long before, as well as triple-bypass heart surgery. I also had a history of developmental disorders, though the doctors had never been able to diagnose fully my particular circumstances. As the months went by I filled out many applications and went to several interviews, but received no offers. Meanwhile, we fasted and prayed that something would open up to help us.

After several months of failure, the state employment agency recommended I contact the veteran's unit. I was a veteran of the Air Force, and they thought one of the veteran's programs might be able to help. I contacted the veteran's unit, as suggested. In turn, they sent me to the local Veterans Administration hospital. Because of my medical and work history, they thought the VA hospital might somehow be able to help with medical care and with rehabilitation training.

The next day I took the bus into town and told the hospital personnel that I had been sent there by the veteran's unit of my local job service. They told me I was truly in luck—it was the last day of a registration window the hospital had been having. If I registered, and if I qualified, I would be able to take full advantage of all the hospital services, without cost. But if I had tried even one day later, they said, I would not have been allowed to apply. (Of course, I didn't consider it luck. I knew it was a wonderful answer to prayer.)

I did qualify. My history was processed into the hospital's data bank, and I was assigned to a set of caseworkers in the various clinics at the hospital. A team of doctors was assigned to work with me, including a regular doctor, a neurologist, and a psychiatrist. They called in other doctors as needed. Since that time, I have used the hospital for all my medical needs. I was assigned to a wonderful counselor who took a great deal of time and trouble to run a variety of tests and come up with the proper diagnosis for my developmental disorders. I also have many physical ailments that have been diagnosed and treated there. In the past year alone, I've had to be admitted to the hospital five times for various serious ailments. They have taken excellent care of me and haven't charged me a cent. There is no insurance premium, no co-payment, no deduction.

The only thing I have to pay for is my medications. Because of my various ailments, I have to take six hundred dollars worth of drugs a month. The medications cost only two dollars per prescription and they mail them to my house. This is a great blessing in itself, because I am unable to drive.

The rehabilitation training never worked out the way I thought it would. But, again with help from the VA hospital, I was able to qualify for Social Security disability payments. I am unable to work for money, but I can work for the Lord. I go to the temple at least one day a week; I work on family history research; and I volunteer at the local Deseret Industries.

I am constantly amazed at how much the Lord has blessed me in these things. My wife and I prayed and placed the problem in his hands. I did all I could to find employment with health insurance, but it wasn't enough. But the Lord, in his love, made up the difference. I know that not everyone who is unemployed or sick gets the kind of blessings I did, but I do know that as we go to the Lord, he will tailor his blessings to suit our true needs.

If thou turn away thy foot . . .
from doing thy pleasure on my holy day;
and call the sabbath a delight, the holy of the Lord, . . .
I will cause thee to ride upon the high places of the earth,
and feed thee with the heritage of Jacob thy father.

ISAIAH 58:13–14

NOT OPEN ON SUNDAY!
QUINTEN AND LARAE WARR,
AS TOLD TO RUTH HEINER

As a young couple, my wife and I worked for several years in Idaho Falls in eating establishments which were open on Sunday. During that time, we noticed that on Sunday, the business often lost money. The machinery always seemed to break down, and then we could not serve the customers. Repairmen charged twice as much on that day. Good hired help was hard to find. We vowed that if we were ever able to buy a business of our own, we would make some changes.

The opportunity finally came one year with the purchase of a drive-in. The loan we took out to buy the business was heavy, and the finance people and the owners of surrounding food establishments assured us that we did not have the slightest chance of paying off our loan if we did not compete on the biggest sales day of the week—Sunday. Because we had already paid the down payment and wanted to make a success of our enterprise we felt trapped. We stayed open.

As predicted, Sunday proved to be our biggest day. Having made the decision to stay open on Sunday, we couldn't change. We were afraid of the business we would lose. Eventually, in the back of our minds, grew the fear that if we did not serve people on Sunday, we would lose our customers and be unable to raise the more than $60,000 we needed to make the business ours.

We had almost reached our goal when I had a heart attack. Because good Sunday help was hard to find, we agreed to close on Sunday from Thanksgiving until Father's Day.

My doctor was pleased with our decision, happy that I could get some much needed rest. But as the months passed, I became worried about the low volume of business we had on our books. One day I told my wife that we should again open on Sunday. She looked at me in silence for several seconds, then said, "First, go look in the mirror and see if you look like a man who could stand seven days of work each week!"

"I guess I don't have to look," I answered slowly. "We'd better forget the whole idea."

Later, as we sat down together to review and evaluate our business year, our fears were confirmed—our gross sales were over $17,000 lower than the previous years! But in spite of our low volume, our balance showed only $10.00 less profit! We were amazed. Pleased with such figures, we agreed to keep the drive-in closed on Sunday for another year. Again, the volume was way down but the profit was no less. Our drive-in was a success without opening on Sunday!

When I think of the poor effect on my health and all the work I did for *nothing* on those Sundays, I am surprised it took me as long to learn the lesson that obedience to the law of the Sabbath carries its own reward. The Sabbath is the Lord's day. We will all be blessed for honoring it.

"Not Open on Sunday!" Quinten and LaRae Warr, as told to Ruth Heiner. Previously published in the *Ensign*, June 1984, 63–64. © by Intellectual Reserve, Inc. Used by permission.

Whosoever repenteth, and hardeneth not his heart,
he shall have claim on mercy through mine Only Begotten Son,
unto a remission of his sins; and these shall enter into my rest.

ALMA 12:34

I WANTED ONE MORE SUMMER OF FUN
TREVOR SANDBERG

I turned nineteen in April of 1992. I had always been active in the Church, was an Eagle Scout, and had attended seminary throughout high school. I planned to go on a mission, but decided to have "one more fun summer" before I went. During that summer, I met a young woman I loved, and we decided to drive to Michigan where she was from. We lived there for a year, married, and had a baby girl. During this time, the Church was not important to me and I fell away.

We moved back to Utah and things started getting rocky between the two of us. I began to acquire "friends" who were bad for me and started to experiment with marijuana and alcohol. I hid these habits from my wife, but the effects were obvious. She soon found out and decided to join with me in my bad decisions. Eight months later, I moved out and shortly thereafter we

Note: This and the following story were written by a son and his mother.

divorced. I fell into depression and started doing drugs more frequently. To fund my lifestyle, I took to stealing, pawning, and even dealing drugs to others. I chose to avoid my family and past friends because I thought they wouldn't understand.

My daughter moved to California with her mother. When she would come to visit my parents, I wouldn't even go see her. I was living a most miserable existence, but I thought I was happy doing "my own thing." Drugs were my master and consumed my thinking and living. For many years I would quit off and on, only to go back to my old friends and that lifestyle. Each time, my parents took me in and loved me, never turning their backs on me.

On New Year's Eve, 1999, I was strung out on crystal meth. I was hanging out with people who had been "up" for weeks on end. One "friend" was so paranoid that he believed someone was trying to kill me. Somebody started a rumor that I was "narking" people off (assisting the police in getting people busted). That was totally false, but in my sleepless and drugged state, it was easy to believe anything. I didn't want to get shot over this misunderstanding, so I decided to hide. I went to an ex-girlfriend's house. I knew she would take me in, but she wasn't home. When I heard a car coming, I ducked inside her garage and stood there in freezing weather for more than two hours, terrified, thinking that people were after me.

It was almost two in the morning when I decided I would rather get shot than freeze to death. I could barely move because I was so cold, but I walked the mile to my sister's home and called her from a gas station a block away. I was out of money and homeless. I felt she was my last hope. I had hit rock bottom.

I had awakened her many times before and she had always let me in. But this time she told me that our mom had told her she shouldn't help me until I helped myself. I was desperate, so I walked to her home anyway and began knocking on the door. Nobody answered. While I continued knocking, a police car pulled up. When the policeman asked what I was doing, I told him that my sister lived there, but that she wasn't answering the door. He told me I was disturbing the peace and proceeded to search me. I had drug paraphernalia on me and some tools I used to fix stereos. Such tools can also be used to break into cars and steal stereos, but I had never used them for that purpose.

I was sitting in the patrol car discussing my problems when my parents pulled up. The policeman let me go with them. They took me to the detox unit, where I slept for five days. I occasionally awoke, ate some food, and went back to sleep. After the fifth day, I called my mom and said I was ready to come home.

It is said that you can't get off crystal meth without rehab— lots and lots of rehab. I was smoking a pack and a half of cigarettes a day, and smoking pot and drinking too. I had finally had enough. I told myself I couldn't do this anymore—that I would soon be dead if I continued. I was miserable!

I quit everything on January 5, 2000—just up and quit! No rehab, no special programs—but lots of prayer and immeasurable help from the Lord. Since then, with many priesthood blessings and continuing pleadings sent up to the Lord, I have stayed clean for more than a year. The Lord blesses and strengthens me every day, helping me to stand firm. I have been certified in computers and now have a good job. I have been so blessed to have my family who have always loved me and are my total support. In fact, I believe it was the power of the prayers of my parents that helped to pull me back from the edge.

I was made an elder in The Church of Jesus Christ of Latter-day Saints on Sunday, February 18, 2001, and was able to baptize my daughter when she turned eight in March. I am so thankful for this priesthood that I now hold.

I am grateful for the gospel and for all that my Savior has done for me. He suffered greatly for me, knowing in advance the terrible course I would take. Then he reached out his loving arms to me, inviting me back. One of his greatest blessings to me and everyone else is the gift of repentance, coupled with the incredible miracle of forgiveness. I pray that I can be an example to help others who have chosen the destructive lifestyle I chose, and show them that there is a way back.

And he will take upon him their infirmities,
that his bowels may be filled with mercy, according to
the flesh, that he may know according to the flesh how
to succor his people according to their infirmities.

ALMA 7:12

A MOTHER'S PRAYER
DARLENE SANDBERG

Trevor is our oldest child and firstborn son whom we love and adore. When he moved out after high school, Mark and I were concerned and frightened. During the last semester of high school, he had begun to make many bad choices and had started sluffing school. He explained that he wanted to "do his own thing." We thought it was a teenage thing, as Trevor had always been such a shy, obedient, loving young man. We found out in the fall that he was living with a girl and we were shocked and dismayed, because we always thought he would serve a mission. Everything seemed to have changed, especially his lifelong goals.

When he turned nineteen, he told us he wanted to have one more fun summer before his mission. We knew at this time that he was not worthy to go, but kept hoping that he would change

Note: This and the preceding story were written by a mother and her son.

his life around and get ready to put his papers in. The night before his best friend's farewell, Trevor and his girlfriend took off for Michigan, where she was from. We were devastated! A few months later Trevor called to tell us that he was going to be a daddy. We were blown away! This shy boy who hardly dated through high school was starting his life like this. We blamed each other; we blamed ourselves; we blamed his friends. We were so confused and angry. How could Heavenly Father let this happen? We were good people. We had family home evening and prayer and scriptures, so why, why was this horrible thing happening to us?

I told Trevor on the phone one day that I wanted him to marry his girlfriend and give his little daughter a name. In December our family flew to Michigan and witnessed through tears and much stress the marriage of Trevor and his very pregnant girlfriend. We watched our lifetime dreams of our son serving a mission go down the drain. Our hearts were as bleak as that cold Michigan landscape.

A few months after the baby's birth, Trevor and his new family moved back to Utah and into our basement. Our granddaughter had a way of easing the pain in our hearts, and all we could do was hope and pray for the best. We soon found out that this was not to be. Our son and his wife, Sarah, were experimenting with alcohol, marijuana, and other drugs. They would leave the baby and go off with their newly acquired friends. His marriage fell apart, and they divorced. Sarah soon remarried and took our sweet granddaughter to California. Our hearts were torn apart once again.

Trevor continued his spiral downhill with drugs and alcohol, stealing from us, pawning the stolen items, and dealing drugs. We slowly became desensitized to all the unbelievable things he had chosen in his life. How could it be that our sweet little boy was making so many bad choices, even dealing drugs? It was so unreal to us.

Depression overtook me, and I pleaded with the Lord to help me understand what I was supposed to learn from this heavy burden. It was so hard to imagine our son out there in that foreign world. Many times we did not know if he was alive or dead. In my self-pity, I blamed myself for not being a good enough mother. What could I have done differently? How could I have instilled in him a stronger testimony to fight the buffetings of the evil one? Why Trevor? Why this pure, innocent baby we had cuddled and rocked and loved? One day I found his patriarchal blessing and read it. I was touched by its power. And I noticed that one part says he will work with wayward youth. I realized then that he would be able to have empathy for those youth *if* and *when* he ever came back.

One day, I was especially depressed and cried out to Heavenly Father, "Are you really there?" The TV was on and Elder Neal A. Maxwell was giving a devotional. Through my tears, I heard the Lord speak to me. He sent peace to my heart. Peace in my trials. Peace in the love of a kind and loving Heavenly Father who knows all of his children. I wrote in my journal that day that I would be able to bear this burden because of my hope in Christ and his love for all his children—whether they be drug addicts or mothers.

That day was a miracle to me. It was a turning point where I was able to let go and let God into my life. I had peace in my heart to believe that Heavenly Father knew Trevor and loved him, and that I could have the faith of a mother and be there when he did come back.

It was more than eight years before Trevor decided he could be worthy of his patriarchal blessing and be able to help those in need. I was filled with joy in my soul, inexpressible, immeasurable joy, when I finally witnessed my son ordained an elder and knew he was worthy to baptize his daughter when she soon turned eight.

Prayers are answered—but not always on our timetable of instant gratification. We learn our lessons along life's way and then in the end, we hear the words whispered, "Peace be unto you."

The burdens which were laid upon Alma
and his brethren were made light;
yea, the Lord did strengthen them that they
could bear up their burdens with ease,
and they did submit cheerfully and with patience
to all the will of the Lord.

MOSIAH 24:15

I PRAYED THAT MY BURDENS WOULD BE LIGHT
TRISHA GORDON

When I received my patriarchal blessing I was interested to see that it said I would have a vocation. It surprised me a bit, because I had always thought I would be a stay-at-home mom with no outside career. I felt the Lord's influence in my choice of a major in college and ended with a business degree. During the years when my husband, Kent, was just getting started in his own career, we thought it would be a blessing if I were to teach business classes at a local junior college. I was usually able to teach classes in the evening when Kent was home so he could be with our young children. I taught two classes a week.

One year the college asked me to teach three classes a week.

And they asked me to teach them in the daytime, which would mean we'd have to find someone else to watch our children while I was at work. I knew the extra money would help our financial situation, but I was troubled by the prospect of the extra hours working—and the hours away from my children. Kent's schedule was also very demanding, with overtime work at his employment and a heavy Church job. Still, I felt I should at least consider the opportunity. Kent and I took it to the Lord, asking him if we should accept the schedule that was being offered to me. As we worked on it and continued to pray, we both felt that it was right for me to teach that schedule, at least for a semester.

Even though I agreed that the Lord's answer was "yes," I was deeply troubled. I already felt pressured in teaching two classes; I already felt that I didn't have enough time for my children and household responsibilities. Now, to teach three classes simply seemed to be too much. It seemed like the new schedule would take my entire week, every week. I felt I would constantly either be preparing for classes or teaching or checking students' work. The burden felt very heavy, and as the days passed I felt overwhelmed, even sorrowful, at the thought of the load I would be carrying.

During the period when I was struggling with these issues, we happened to read in family scripture time the story of Alma and his people when they were in bondage to the Lamanites.

"And it came to pass that so great were their afflictions that they began to cry mightily to God. . . . And it came to pass that the voice of the Lord came to them in their afflictions, saying:

Lift up your heads and be of good comfort, for I . . . will also ease the burdens which are put upon your shoulders, that even you cannot feel them upon your backs, even while you are in bondage. . . . And now it came to pass that the burdens which were laid upon Alma and his brethren were made light; yea, the Lord did strengthen them that they could bear up their burdens with ease, and they did submit cheerfully and with patience to all the will of the Lord" (Mosiah 24:10, 13–15).

That's the blessing I want! I said to myself. *If I can't have this burden removed from me, maybe the Lord will help it to feel light.* I didn't say anything to Kent about the secret feelings of my heart, but in my private, prayerful yearning, I asked the Lord if he might bless me as he blessed Alma and his people. But still the heavy feelings continued.

Not long after that I asked Kent to give me a priesthood blessing, hoping it might give me peace. I sat on a chair in our bedroom and he placed his hands on my head. He said a number of things that were comforting, though I don't specifically remember what they were. Then he said something I will never forget: "And I declare unto you that you will receive a blessing like Heavenly Father gave to the Nephites of old, when they were in bondage to the Lamanites. Your burdens will be made light by the power of the Lord."

I was very surprised to hear those words—and both grateful and relieved. The blessing was realized almost immediately. We went to bed shortly after the blessing—and when I woke up the next morning, I felt different. My burdens had been lifted and were gone. And my relief continued through that entire term.

As the term progressed, I noticed another blessing: the children did very well with my new schedule. They didn't seem to suffer from by absences. Things ran even more smoothly at home than normal. The Lord truly blessed me and my family in my extra time away from home—because we were doing his will.

The voice of the Lord came into my mind.

ENOS 1:10

"STOP AND SEE YOUR DAD"
JOHN W. MARKHAM

Toward the end of his life, my dad had to spend some time in the hospital because of cancer. I was serving in the stake presidency at the time and would drive past the hospital to and from my meetings. I would typically leave for my meeting early so I could stop at the hospital to spend some time with my father.

One evening I had a nice visit with him. He seemed to be doing fairly well and I left him resting and went on to the stake center for my meeting. The meeting lasted until after 11 P.M. I was very tired and thinking how nice it would be to get home. As I passed the hospital I noticed that most of the lights were out and the hospital seemed to be dark and quiet for the night. But as I drove on by, the still small voice said, "Stop and see your dad." I thought to myself, "I don't need to stop. I just spent some time with him a few hours ago."

A second time the voice said, "Stop and see your dad." I argued with myself about how it was not necessary to see him again.

By this time I was well past the hospital. A third time the

voice repeated, "Stop and see your dad." I turned the car around and drove back to the hospital. All was very quiet in the halls. I took the elevator up to the third floor. As I stepped out of the elevator I could hear someone moaning and crying because he was in so much pain. As I walked down the hall the moans grew louder, and I began to realize that the cries were coming from my dad's room. When Dad saw me he grabbed hold of my hands and said, "Can you help me?" He said he was in a great deal of pain and that the nurse would not give him anything for it.

I hurried to find the head nurse, but she wouldn't budge. "Your father cannot have another pain shot for an hour and twenty minutes," she said. "We don't want him to become addicted to the medicine."

I responded, "Dad is not going to live much longer. I don't think addiction is an issue. I thought the doctor said he could have a shot for pain any time he needed it."

The doctor and I were personal friends, so I went to the phone in the nurses' station and called him and got him out of bed. It was now past midnight. When the doctor answered the phone I said, "Doctor, will you please listen to this?" I then held the phone up so he could hear the crying.

The doctor said, "That sounds like someone in a great deal of pain."

I said, "That's my dad and they will not give him anything for the pain he's in." The doctor asked to speak to the head nurse. When she hung up the phone, she asked for Dad's nurse to come to the nurses' station. She told the nurse to write on Dad's chart that he was to have pain medication any time he needed it and that she was to give him some right now.

I stayed with Dad a while longer, rubbing his back and talking to him. In fifteen or twenty minutes he fell asleep and I left him sleeping soundly. The next day Dad told my mother about me coming to visit him close to midnight. "How did John know that I needed him so badly?" he asked.

But I have my own questions: What if I hadn't listened to that small voice prompting me? and Why did the voice have to speak to me three times?

How excellent is thy lovingkindness, O God!
therefore the children of men put their trust
under the shadow of thy wings.

PSALM 36:7

THE LORD GAVE ME MY JOBS
SUZANNE FENSTERMAKER

I never wanted to work outside the home. Even as a little girl I just wanted to be a wife and mother. The prophets supported this, of course. After I married, when we struggled financially I would do baby-sitting or other things I could do at home.

When we moved to Arizona, things got especially bad. My husband, Alan, was unable to keep a good job, and we repeatedly had to receive help from our families and from the Church. After we had lived there for about a year, my brother called me and told me about a job working in a video store. They needed some help, he said, and all I had to do was call them and I would be hired. With much trepidation (and after prayer) I made the call, went in, had a short interview, and they put me right to work. I started out sweeping the floor and ended up an office supervisor. Working gave me confidence that I had lacked before.

I quit after four and a half years because Alan finally had a good job. Unfortunately, that good job ended about four months after I quit my own job at the video store. We prayed fervently for help. I hoped and expected that something would come through for Alan. But a couple of weeks later a lady in our ward called and told me that she had been offered a part-time job at the elementary school but she couldn't take it. If I was interested, she said, all I had to do was call the principal and then go fill out an application at the district office.

We prayed carefully about the possibility and felt that this was an opportunity from the Lord. I applied and was hired just as my friend had said. I worked two hours a day the first year, then three and a half hours from then on. I went from being the recess aide to working as a part-time tutor for kids who were struggling with reading and/or math. It was perfect, because I was home with my family but still contributing to the family income. When I quit working at the video store, I had promised my children that as long as they were still in school, I wouldn't take another full-time job, and I was able to keep my promise.

The first summer off was very challenging, though, because we didn't have my income at all in the summer. We continued to pray for help. The very next year, a lady called and asked if I would like to work at the snack bar at the community swimming pool. It filled in part of the gap, but we were still struggling—and praying. Some time afterwards, I was asked to help do research on a long-term book project. This project lasted well over five years and paid well. I was able to work at home and research articles from the leaders of the Church, so it was also spiritually uplifting.

After I had worked for the school eleven years, for the pool three years, and for the book project five years, my husband was able to apply for Social Security disability. He was approved, but the income we'd receive from that would not by any means be enough to get us by. I kept feeling like maybe the time had come for me to get a full-time job, but I resisted it even though all the children were grown up. When I was working at the school one day I saw the weekly newsletter that lists job openings in the district. The Spirit pushed me to apply for two of them.

I actually got called in for interviews but made a total fool of myself because of my lack of knowledge of job interviews. However, the receptionist in the personnel department was a friend of mine, and I asked her how I could improve. She gave me some very helpful suggestions. A few weeks later I was prompted again to apply for a job, and that time I was hired. After eight months I applied for a better job in the district and got it.

I never would have gone out on my own to look for a job if the Spirit hadn't pushed me in that direction. I desired too strongly to be at home taking care of my children. I still struggle being a full-time employee, but I know I am where I am meant to be at this time. And I can say truthfully that the Lord has literally given me every job I have ever had.

He that findeth his life shall lose it:
and he that loseth his life for my sake shall find it.

—MATTHEW 10:39

WHAT CAN I DO TO BE HAPPY?
ALLAN K. BURGESS AND MAX H. MOLGARD

The family sat around the bed in the hospital room where their mother was dying. They had been told that she had only a few hours to live. Allan, who was the oldest child, looked around the room at the faces of his family. His father, who seemed to be under control, was sitting across from him. Allan knew that all of them loved his mother very much and wondered what they were thinking about. His own thoughts went back over her life and the great courage she had shown even though she had been bedridden and in constant pain for the last ten to fifteen years.

His mother's back had been broken in several places, and, because of complications from other problems, it would never heal. This meant that she had to be in bed in constant traction in order to lessen the pain as much as possible.

Allan remembered one day that his mother had been depressed and had asked him to come over and talk to her. She wanted to know what she could do so that she wouldn't be depressed. Even though she was in pain she wanted to be happy.

Allan didn't know what to tell her, so he said that he would fast and pray about it and talk to her again the next Sunday.

The answer that Allan received shocked him and he didn't know how he was going to tell his mother. When Sunday arrived, Allan sat down with his mother and told her that she was being too selfish and only thinking of herself. What she needed to do, if she was going to be happy, was to quit worrying about her problems and start helping other people. She asked Allan how she could help others when she was in bed twenty-four hours a day. Allan really didn't know the answer to that problem and told her that he had given her the solution but it was up to her to figure out how to do it.

Now Allan remembered how his mother had responded to the Lord's answer and had filled her life with service for others. Allan's father would bring her the ingredients and she would prepare meals lying flat on her back in bed. She put up fruit and Allan's dad cooked it. She called volunteer agencies and found things that she could do to help others. She called people daily that were lonely and needed cheering up. She made gifts and had her husband deliver them. She taught a Primary class in her living room, which was possible because she lived close to the chapel.

A few weeks after she started to serve others in this way, she grabbed Allan by the hand and thanked him with tears in her eyes for giving her the guidance she needed to be happy. She told him that, at first, she wondered how she could do what the Lord had indicated. She then exercised her faith and said to herself, "If the Lord said I could do it then I can do it," and she started looking for ways to serve.

Burgess and Molgard, *Stories That Teach Gospel Principles*, 41–42.

I will also be your light in the wilderne
and I will prepare the way before you
if it so be that ye shall keep my commandmer
and ye shall know that it is by me that ye ar

1 NEPHI 17:13

THE CONTACT LENS
RICHARD H. CRACROFT

There are a multitude of patterns which frame the finger of the Lord in our lives and bring His ways and means into focus. One of the patterns that has guided me in exercising personal faith first smacked me in the right eye as a young missionary. President Harold B. Lee named it best when he taught us to "walk to the edge of the light, and perhaps a few steps into the darkness, and you will find that the light will appear and move ahead of you." That step into the dark is the start-up key to an act of faith. Thus the brother of Jared prepared sixteen stones and, from the darkness of mortality but with the brightness of faith, asked, "Touch these stones, O Lord, with thy finger, and prepare them that they may shine forth in darkness" (Ether 3:4). And the Lord flooded Mahonri Moriancumer (the real name of the brother of Jared) and his people with light. It is a pattern: faith precedes the

cle, as darkness precedes dawn—just as it did when Peter for-
got himself and stepped out of that ship and into the darkness to
walk upon the sea (see Matthew 14:29); just as it did recently
when I, as home teacher, taught the "One Step into the Dark
Pattern" to a large and faithful family by blindfolding the four-
year-old daughter, standing her on a table, and asking her to fall
off the table into the waiting arms of her daddy. Without a
moment's hesitation, and despite the obvious squeamishness of
her older brothers and sisters, the little girl stood tall and fell
headlong into the darkness—where she was safely caught by her
father. She had taken that step into the dark—and was duly
rewarded by a glad (and relieved) home teacher.

So it was for me, when, on a rainy summer afternoon in 1958,
I unwittingly traced the "One Step into the Dark Pattern" while
tracting along a gravel road on a hillside above Baden,
Switzerland. As we walked from home to home, I was suddenly
laid low by a speck of dust in my right eye. I learned, as one who
had worn brand-new contact lenses for only five days, that a mote
feels like a beam. I quickly extracted the lens, cleaned and rewet-
ted it, and prepared to reinsert it. But as I held my finger at the
ready, a gust of wind suddenly swept the lens from my fingertip:
My lens was gone with the wind. I stood aghast—and virtually
blind, being plunged instantly into 20/600 vision in one eye,
which had been miraculously corrected to 20/20 only a week
earlier.

Elder Neil Reading and I began to search on hands and knees
in the wet gravel, sweeping an eight-foot radius from my supposed

point of loss. We searched futilely for twenty minutes. Then, half-blind and half-despairing, I suggested to my companion that while we were already in position, we should pray. I reasoned with the Lord, told him about my need to see; about our need to meet our three investigator families that evening; about my feeling that there was more to be gained by finding the lens than by my learning whatever I was to learn from the loss. As I concluded the prayer and stood up, I received one of those Joseph Smith "flashes of intelligence." It surprised me, but I reacted at once. Explaining the revealed plan to my startled companion, I stood on my feet in the same place I had stood earlier, squeezed out my left contact lens, and was instantly plunged into the distorted, virtual blindness of 20/600 vision. I had begun my step into the dark.

Assured that my companion was on his knees and at the ready, I put my left lens in my mouth, extracted it, and, mounting it on my finger some six inches from my face, I waited—but not for long. A slight breeze caught my left lens, and it was gone. My step into the dark was now complete. I stood stock-still, heart in throat, until Elder Reading said, "I see it. It's still in the air."

"Don't lose it," I pled, and held my breath.

"It's still up," he whispered, now ten feet away. Then, from even further away, he exclaimed, "It's starting to fall!"

"Keep your eye on it," I pled again, wringing my hands in apprehension.

"I see it! I see it!" he said. There was a long pause—of three hours or seconds—and then. "Oh, my gosh! Oh, my gosh!"

I braced.

"Oh, my gosh," he repeated; "it's landed, and"—pause . . .
pause . . . pause—" . . . almost right on top of the other lens!"

"You see the other lens?" I shouted.

"Yes, it's right here!"

The darkness was flooded with light.

Unable to see a thing, I crawled over to him on hands and
knees. Slowly, he planted in my palm, in order, my left and right
lenses—my seer stones. I wet the lenses and, with my back to the
wind and sheltered by my companion's hovering frame, I
implanted them: "And there was light, and it was good." And we
knelt, full of gratitude, and I thanked our God for tender and tan-
gible mercies. We pressed on to the next house, filled with wonder
at a God who knows each sparrow's fall *and* the exact where-
abouts in Baden, Switzerland, of Elder Cracroft's right contact
lens.

From "Tracing Father's Patterns: 'Taking One Step into the Dark,'" in Goddard and Cracroft, *My Soul
Delighteth in the Scriptures*, 37–39.

If they humble themselves before me, and have faith in me,
then will I make weak things become strong unto them.

ETHER 12:27

HE SHOWED ME MY
HIDDEN WEAKNESSES
REBEKAH ISAACSON

Once we had a lesson in Gospel Doctrine class about the promise in Ether 12:27: "If men come unto me I will show unto them their weakness. . . . If they humble themselves before me, and have faith in me, then will I make weak things become strong unto them." I suspect my response to that lesson was similar to that of many other people. I knew I was far from perfect, but I wasn't sure specifically what the Lord wanted me to do differently. I was temple-worthy and active in the Church. I felt I was loving and even-tempered with my family. My husband and I were faithful in having family home evening, family scripture reading, and family prayer with our children. I never missed visiting teaching and tried to do quiet compassionate service on the side. I tried to be prayerful in my life and to follow the promptings of the Spirit. But I knew that I had plenty I needed to do better, or do differently, if I could just put my finger on it.

I decided to fast and pray, seeking the Lord's guidance on what he wanted me to do. What unseen weaknesses did I have that were keeping me from being all he needed me to be? I was fearful of what he might tell me, but felt that I *had* to know. I prayed throughout my fast, and then prayed again when I ended my fast, asking the Lord to reveal my weaknesses to me. I felt the Spirit present in my prayers, but didn't feel any specific response to my question. I decided that maybe the Lord didn't have anything to tell me on that subject.

But my efforts opened a door that had been closed. Throughout the weeks and months that followed my eyes were opened, and I saw my innermost heart more clearly; I saw myself more as the Lord sees me. I saw that the outward person—the one who is doing so much right—often doesn't reflect who we really are. I saw a great weakness of pride that I hadn't recognized before. I saw an unrighteous need and desire to control others that I hadn't been aware of.

Recognizing what I needed to work on was half the battle. The next step was to seek his help in making those weak things become strengths in me. I knew that I must do so with humility and faith. The results have not come overnight. But as I remain humble and teachable, and as I continue to seek the help of the Lord, he is helping me to progress in these areas. By walking with him, by relying on him—and then by doing all I possibly can myself—I can continue on the path toward perfection.

Cast your mind upon the night that you
cried unto me in your heart. . . .
Did I not speak peace to your mind?

D&C 6:22–23

THE LIGHT THAT LEADETH ME BACK
LAUREN A. DICK

February of 1997 found my husband and myself in Phoenix, Arizona, where we had flown for a business seminar and a few days' getaway. On our first night away from home, I knelt beside the bed, swallowed up in my thoughts of a message we had received just an hour before. The message was overwhelming. There had been an accident in the Philippines involving our oldest son, Tony, who was serving the twentieth month of his mission there. He was now lying in a coma in a hospital on the other side of the world. As I knelt there, all my being yearned to plead with Heavenly Father to bring my son back to me, to make him well and whole. I wanted to hear Tony's laughter, to see him walk, run, play his clarinet, and do all the things he had always done. But I couldn't ask. Something held me back. After kneeling there for a long while, I simply prayed, "Dear Heavenly Father, I have trained and nurtured him. I brought him up to be thy servant. He is thine. I give him back to thee. I will accept thy will." In the very moment I said these words, it was as though Heavenly Father wrapped his arms around me. I felt the most beautiful, indescribable peace. I knew then that whatever happened, things would be all right. For the next few days, we quietly but anxiously awaited a daily report of our son's condition. Each day the report remained very much the same.

One week after receiving the news of the accident, following a twenty-one-hour flight, I arrived in Manila at 9:15 P.M. Elder and Sister Richardson from the Missionary Receiving Center met me at the airport, and we went directly to the hospital where Tony had lain motionless in his coma for more than a week. I had intended to see Tony only briefly that night. But when I walked into that hospital room and saw him lying there so silent and still, both his head and body bruised and swollen, tubes and wires coming out of him everywhere, I could not leave. I spoke to him, expressing my love for him. "Mom is here," I said. "I'm going to stay."

I held his hands and stroked his cheeks. There was no response. For hours I stood, speaking between long moments of quiet. I lifted and rubbed his limbs, all the while telling him about our family, his brothers and sisters, speaking their names over and over, hoping for even the smallest response. There was none. Early in the morning as I stood at his bedside weeping quietly, I felt prompted to sing to him. Tony loved music. When he was a small child, he loved me to sing Primary songs as lullabies. There, in the wee hours of the morning, as I held his hand, I started singing very softly, "I Am a Child of God," beginning with the first verse. As I neared the end of the third verse, tears began to fall from Tony's eyes, rolling down the sides of his face, filling his ears. Ever so gently I reached with my free hand to wipe the tears from his ears, and as I did, his hand squeezed mine. *He was there!*

At that moment I remembered the morning following the accident. My husband and I had slept very soundly. Sleep found us as soon as our heads were laid upon the pillows. The peace we felt was very comforting. Early the next morning, however, I was awakened as suddenly as if I had been shaken. There in front of me I envisioned my son Tony, standing behind the pulpit in our chapel. I heard him giving his homecoming address. The vision faded, and I thought, "This was a witness telling me my son would come home whole and well!"

For the next few days, as I pondered what I had seen and heard, a scripture kept trying to emerge in my mind, but I could not recall it exactly. I wanted so much to read it, but my scriptures were not there with me. I had neglected to pack them when we had left home, a mistake I hope I never make again. When we did arrive home, I quickly found my scriptures and read Doctrine and Covenants 6:22–24: "Verily, verily, I say unto you, if you desire a further witness, cast your mind upon the night that you cried unto me in your heart, that you might know concerning the truth of these things. Did I not speak peace to your mind concerning the matter? What greater witness can you have than from God? And now, behold, you have received a witness; for if I have told you things which no man knoweth have you not received a witness?" This scripture fanned the flame of my faith. Day after day and night after night as I stood by my son's bedside and watched him slowly work his way back to life, it brought back the witness I had seen and heard.

The doctors were at times pessimistic. Some did not believe he would ever fully recover. Others believed, and told us, that he would never walk again. Through it all I continued to tell them that I knew he would be well and whole. They would look at me sympathetically and shake their heads.

One month after I arrived in Manila, Tony and I flew home. He came home with the aid of a wheelchair, not having sat for more than twenty minutes on his own and having made no attempt at all to stand. Within a day of arriving at our home, we took Tony to LDS Hospital in Salt Lake City to spend (we were told) at least four to six weeks in a rehabilitation center. Miraculously, within five days—on the very day that Tony's younger brother was to leave Salt Lake City to fly to the Philippines to begin his own mission there—Tony was walking the halls of the rehabilitation center with only one cane to assist him. At 5:30 that morning, we picked up Tony to join our family in seeing his brother off. While experiencing that sweet reunion at the airport with my husband and all of my six children, I felt the light from my lamp growing brighter once again.

4 July 1997

Tony drove to Salt Lake City yesterday. President Snell, Tony's mission president, and his wife are returning home today. Tony would have returned home with them on this day also had he not had his accident. I can't help but think it is as though he has, in fact, just now returned to us. The evidence of his injuries and ordeal is now barely perceptible, except for a slight limp in his left leg, and this will improve with time. As I was thinking of the great miracle that has occurred in our lives in the past five months, I turned again to Doctrine and Covenants 6. This time I read verse 36: "Look unto me in every thought; doubt not, fear not."

Thy Word Is a Lamp: Women's Stories of Finding Light, 88–91.

Ask God, the Eternal Father, in the name of Christ,
if these things are not true; and if ye shall ask with
a sincere heart, with real intent, having faith in Christ,
he will manifest the truth of it unto you,
by the power of the Holy Ghost.

MORONI 10:4

"YOU ALREADY KNOW"
TANDEA FORD

When I read the Book of Mormon as a teenager, I would often read a verse or a passage and my heart would say, "Yes!" I would read "I will go and do the things which the Lord hath commanded," and I would feel a thrill in my heart. I would read, "Counsel with the Lord in all thy doings, and he will direct thee for good," and I would feel comforted that I could be so directed. I would read about Jesus and his visitation to the Nephites and marvel that a ring of fire encircled the children and that angels ministered to them.

One day during my sophomore year, my seminary teacher shared with us the story about when he had prayed and felt the truth of the Book of Mormon. He hadn't sought that testimony until he was on his mission. He urged us to not wait that long, but to pray now, if we hadn't, and ask Heavenly Father to tell us if the Book of Mormon was true.

I was unsure how an answer from Heavenly Father would feel. I didn't know how to recognize it if it did come. But I thought it was time for me to begin to learn how to communicate with my Father in Heaven. I decided that praying about the Book of Mormon was probably the best place to start. So I prayed and asked Heavenly Father if the Book of Mormon was true. I didn't feel a strong "yes" or a strong "no" in response. I didn't feel a burning or a stupor. I wasn't sure what I felt.

But as I pondered the feeling in my heart, it seemed as though Heavenly Father said to me, "You already know the Book of Mormon is true."

A few days later I prayed and asked Heavenly Father if that answer was from him and if it was true. I felt it was. He was giving credit and validity to all those times when, in reading the Book of Mormon, I had a good feeling, a confirming feeling from the Spirit. He was telling me that he had answered my prayer even before I had prayed it.

Is any sick among you? let him call for the elders of the church;
and let them pray over him, anointing him
with oil in the name of the Lord:
And the prayer of faith shall save the sick,
and the Lord shall raise him up.

JAMES 5:14–15

THE SIGNAL THE DOCTORS NEEDED
RICHARD T. SOWELL

One Sunday morning when I was serving as bishop many years ago, I was approached by Bishop Lou Stephenson (who was the bishop of the ward that shared our building). He said, "I have just received a call from the hospital. They have a girl there who wants to be administered to by the Mormon priesthood. Do you have anyone who can go with me?" I told him that I was free and would be glad to go with him.

When we arrived at the hospital we were told two girls had been injured in a one-car accident in the desert about fifty miles away. They had been thrown from their car and had lain out in the winter weather for most of the night. Finally a truck driver had noticed the car and found the two girls. He called for help, and they were brought to our hospital in Nampa, Idaho.

The emergency room where the girls were was bustling with activity. Doctors and nurses were rushing in and out with great concern on their faces. The hospital was run by the Catholic Sisters of Mercy. The sister in charge told the supervising doctor that the "men from the church are here." The doctor answered brusquely that they were very busy with these two girls; if we must come into the emergency room, he said, we were to quickly do what we had to do and to stay out of the way.

The girls were on tables a few feet apart. One girl was covered with dried blood and had many cuts and bruises. She was a mess. The other girl looked to be unconscious, but didn't seem to be cut up so badly. The medical team was focused on the girl who appeared to be hurt so badly. We went first to the other girl and spoke to her, asking her name, but we didn't expect a response. She was able to whisper her name. One of us anointed her with oil. Then, as we gently rested our hands on her head to seal the anointing, she abruptly sat straight up, and projected the most vile black fluid from her mouth across the room. I was amazed at the force with which she vomited that black liquid.

Startled, the medical team immediately left the first girl and came to where we were. Bishop Stephenson and I stepped out of the way. One of the doctors said, "This girl is badly hurt. She's bleeding internally, and if we don't act fast she could bleed to death."

We moved across the room, administered to the first girl, and then left the hospital to return to our meetings. Later in the day we learned that the girl who had been covered with blood had experienced primarily surface injuries and would recover very quickly. The second girl was indeed badly hurt internally and could have bled to death while the doctors worked on her friend. The doctors agreed that if she hadn't thrown up when she did, they wouldn't have known the extent of her injuries. It seemed clear that her vomiting when we were giving her the blessing had most likely saved her life. It took some time for her to heal, but she did heal and was able to go on the mission that she had been preparing for.

What a blessing it was that these girls had the presence of mind to ask for a priesthood blessing. And what a great blessing that the Lord, through a priesthood administration of two of his sons, enabled the girl's body to send the doctors the very signal they needed so they could respond to her injuries and save her life.

I was led by the Spirit, not knowing beforehand
the things which I should do.

1 NEPHI 4:6

WE RUSHED HIM TO THE HOSPITAL
J. C. AARONS

I was coming back from a trip to the Grand Canyon with my dad and grandpa, and we stopped at a service station to get some gas and to stretch our legs. Grandpa was getting pretty old, and his eyes were very bad. He went into the station, and when he came back he tripped and fell against a metal sign standing near the door. The frame of the sign gashed through his right arm, cutting it deeply. I tried to stop the bleeding while we rushed him to the hospital.

While we were in the emergency room of the hospital, Dad wanted to give Grandpa a blessing. "Go ask a nurse if she knows how to get hold of any Mormon elders," Dad said. I went out to the desk and relayed the request.

"I'm sorry," the nurse said. "I don't know any Mormons."

But before she had even finished her sentence a man stepped up from behind me and said, "I'm a Mormon elder. I can help."

The man assisted Dad in giving the blessing, and then began

to leave. "You were here at just the right time," Dad said. "If you were here visiting a loved one, I hope they'll be all right."

"Oh, no," the man answered. "I don't know anyone here."

"Then why did you come in the first place?" Dad asked.

"I was driving through the neighborhood and I just got the feeling that I was needed here."

The Lord knew about our need even before we had expressed it—and had the solution in place.

Thus saith the Lord God of Israel,
That which thou hast prayed to me . . . I have heard.

2 KINGS 19:20

"ADAMS, HOW DO YOU DO IT?"
PETER C. ADAMS

Shortly after my mission I was drafted into the army. The war in Vietnam was going strong, but Congress had recently passed a law allowing draftees to enlist instead in a National Guard or Reserve unit. I was anxious to continue my university education and took that option. I enlisted in the Air National Guard and went to basic training at Lackland Air Force Base in San Antonio, Texas.

I was worried when I went. Friends and acquaintances seemed eager to tell me horror stories of "boot camp." The drill instructors (DIs) were abusive, they said. DIs went out of their way to harass their trainees; the DIs would use a lot of profanity and would "get in your face," doing everything they could to break you down. The other trainees, as a rule, would be crude and rough.

It seemed particularly hard to go from the sweet and gentle mission atmosphere to the worldly setting of boot camp. I prayed before I went that I would be able to adjust well without lowering my standards. I prayed further that I would be a good example to both my fellow airmen and to the DIs.

On my first day I discovered that there were two other Mormons in our eighty-man squad (officially called a *flight*). By the third day one of the three had been transferred out, leaving just two of us. We were assigned to bunks on opposite ends of the floor, so I didn't have a lot of opportunity to spend time with my fellow Mormon.

On my first night I wondered if I should kneel by my bed and say a prayer. I finally decided that I would say my prayer while lying on my bunk. But after the lights were off I heard a young Baptist kid two bunks over kneel on the floor. I repented and did the same every night thereafter.

The training was rough, just as my friends had predicted. I wasn't in the best of shape physically, and the running and other exercise was demanding. Nor have I ever considered myself particularly coordinated, and the close-ranks marching required quite a bit of concentration. I did better with the classroom work; I was able to quickly pick up on the material they were teaching us, and I did well with the tests.

We had two primary DIs assigned to our flight. From the very first day they started a "good guy-bad guy" routine with us. One would be tough and coarse and demanding, while the other would be nice to us. Then the next day they would reverse roles, trying to keep us off balance. Rather than watch for what we did well, they seemed to watch for us to make a mistake. They took pride in giving out demerit slips ("gigs") for even the smallest infraction. Those who got gig slips had to pull extra guard duty or extra kitchen duty—or they could even have their Sunday privileges removed from them.

We didn't get any leave time for the first several weeks, but after the first Sunday we were allowed to take a couple of hours to attend the church meeting of our choice, which was held at the base chapel. Sundays became my oasis. I would walk over to the little chapel and meet with a number of other LDS airmen; the meetings were conducted by an LDS chaplain. Often the missionaries attended as well. The other LDS fellow in my flight joined me in trying to get some of our new friends to attend church with us, but few were willing to. Time off was so precious that most of the men felt they had other things to do with their short break.

As the weeks went by the men kept track of those in our flight who still hadn't received any gigs. After a couple of weeks there were only a half dozen of us left. Then, one by one, the DIs found cause to give out gigs to those who hadn't received them. Eventually only one man in the eighty-man flight hadn't received a single demerit—me. The other airmen watched me from day to day, wondering how I did it. The DIs continued to give out gigs freely. Even those who tried hard not to get one continued to slip up one way or another. Gigs were given for not marching correctly, for slacking off during a run, for not having shoes shined, for not standing properly at attention, for talking when we were supposed to be silent, for averting our eyes when the DI was yelling at us, for not making our beds exactly right, for not having our foot lockers properly arranged, and so forth.

"Adams, how do you do it?" the airmen began to ask me, first one, then another, then a third. "It's impossible not to get a single gig."

I just smiled. They knew I was a Mormon. They knew I didn't smoke, drink, or swear. I had prayed that the Lord would help me to be a good example to the other men, and he was answering my prayer in a surprising way. I'm not one who likes to be in the limelight, but the Lord wanted to set me up as a light on a hill for those other airmen to see.

In our last week the flight was given the opportunity to send two airmen to a special competition to choose the best airman from our entire class. One of the two airmen was appointed by our DIs. The other was chosen by popular vote, using a secret ballot. I was almost unanimously selected by the airmen in my barracks. "Why did you pick Adams?" the DIs asked. The answer: "He's the best airman we've got. He's never gotten a single gig."

The DIs were surprised; they couldn't understand how they had failed to give me my full share of demerits. They watched me closer during that last week, trying to find an excuse to give me a gig slip. The Lord continued to help me, and I was able to complete my time in boot camp without receiving a demerit.

I did not win the competition for top airman of our class. I wasn't able to bring any of my new associates into the Church. But I was able to plant some seeds among all the other men in my flight; I was able to be an example for them as well as for my drill instructors. The Lord helped me through that experience with the sustaining influence of his Spirit, blessing me according to the prayers of my heart.

The Lord doth . . . gathereth together the outcasts of Israel.
He healeth the broken in heart, and bindeth up their wounds.

PSALM 147:2–3

SHE DUG THE GRAVE WITH HER FINGERS
FREDERICK W. BABBEL

[In Karlsruhe, Germany, just after World War II, I saw] a somewhat timid and emaciated sister. She had burlap sacks wrapped around her feet and legs in place of shoes. Even these were now in shreds. Her clothing was patched and tattered. As I looked at her purple-grey face, her swollen red eyes and protruding joints, I was told that I was looking at a person in the advanced stages of starvation. President [Max] Zimmer acquainted me with her hardships and incredible testimony.

This good sister had lived in East Prussia. During the final days of the frightful battles in that area, her husband had been killed. She was left with four small children, one of them a babe in arms. Under the agreements of the occupying military powers, she was one of 11 million Germans who was required to leave her homeland and all her basic possessions, and go to Western Germany to seek a new home. She was permitted only to take such bare necessities, bedding, etc. as she could load into her small wooden-wheeled wagon—about sixty-five pounds in all—

which she pulled across this desolate wasteland of war. Her smallest child she carried in her arms while the other small children did their best to walk beside her during this trek of over a thousand miles on foot.

She started her journey in late summer. Having neither food nor money among her few possessions, she was forced to gather a daily subsistence from the fields and forests along the way. Constantly she was also faced with dangers from panicky refugees and marauding troops.

Soon the snows came and temperatures dropped to about 40 degrees below zero. One by one her children died, either frozen to death or the victims of starvation or both. She buried them in shallow graves by the roadside, using a tablespoon as a shovel. Finally, as she was reaching the end of her journey, her last little child died in her arms. Her spoon was gone now, so she dug a grave in the frozen earth with her bare fingers.

As she was recalling these and other difficulties at a testimony meeting, she explained that her grief at that moment became unbearable. Here she was kneeling in the snow at the graveside of her last child. She had now lost her husband and all her children. She had given up all her earthly goods, her home, and even her homeland. She found herself among people whose condition resembled her own wretched state of affairs.

In this moment of deep sorrow and bewilderment, she felt her heart would break. In despair she contemplated how she might end her own life as so many of her fellow countrymen were doing.

How easy it would be to jump off a nearby bridge, she thought, or to throw herself in front of an oncoming train!

Then she testified that as these thoughts assailed her, something within her said, "Get down on your knees and pray." And she then rapturously explained how she prayed more fervently than she had ever prayed before.

In conclusion, she bore a glorious testimony, stating that of all ailing people in her saddened land she was one of the happiest because she knew that God lived, that Jesus is the Christ, and that if she continued faithful and true to the end she would be saved in the celestial kingdom of God.

Babbel, *On Wings of Faith,* 40–42. Used by permission.

Thou calledst in trouble, and I delivered thee.

PSALM 81:7

DELIVERANCE FROM A CLIFF
ORLANDO T. BARROWES

When I was fourteen I became intrigued with circus-type acrobatics. I talked my younger brother and some of my friends into practicing with me. We spent many hours and days "performing" at home in my yard.

That same summer I was excited when my neighbor invited me and my younger brother to hike Timpanogos Mountain with him and his son, who was eleven years old.

The day came. We started hiking. Soon we boys became restless with the slow pace of my neighbor and another man who had come with us, and we began to move ahead. Soon we were far ahead of the adults. We passed the lake and the glacier and went around toward the peak. As we turned a corner we found ourselves on a ledge that led along the face of a cliff. Instead of leading up toward the peak as we expected, it became narrower and narrower. Eventually we found ourselves hugging the cliff wall, the ledge having tapered down to nothing.

We thought about going back, but it didn't seem possible.

We looked down on the drop-off of some one hundred feet, where there was another small ledge, and then another drop.

As we considered our plight, my eleven-year-old friend began to cry. We decided to pray because we really were in extreme danger. After the prayer we felt quite calm—and we began to understand how to get out of our predicament.

Even though we could see only about two feet above our heads, we felt that the trail had to be above us. But how to get up there? We realized we could use our much-practiced acrobatic skills.

My younger brother scaled up me, stood on my shoulders, and then locked his hands around a big rock. He struggled over the top. About a minute later he informed us that he had found the trail.

My young friend then climbed up my back and stood on my shoulders. My brother reached down from above, grabbed him, and hoisted him up. Then the two of them formed a chain with a rock for an anchor. One of them leaned down far enough so that I could reach his leg and I pulled myself up on top, using him as a rope. It still scares me to think about it! Twenty minutes later we were at the mountain's summit. We couldn't have been more thankful and relieved to be safe and alive.

I have been up that mountain several times since, and I have observed how unbelievably treacherous it was to be where we were and do what we did. To this day I continue to be thankful that our Heavenly Father was mindful of three unwise boys, that he heard their prayer, calmed their fears, and helped them out of a very tight spot!

Be humble, and be submissive and gentle; easy to be entreated;
full of patience and long-suffering.

ALMA 7:23

GOD AND I WERE OF ONE MIND
BONNIE BALLIF-SPANVILL

In the last few years, I have lost five of those most dear to me: my eldest sister, my eldest brother, my mother, my father, and most recently my husband. Before his death, my husband was very ill and nearly died on several occasions. I often went to my Heavenly Father to try to understand, to keep my vision clear, to keep from sinking into valleys of despair. Let me share one of the many experiences I had that helped me see my situation more clearly.

On one occasion, my husband went into the hospital for a transfusion. While he was receiving the second unit of blood, he went into a coma. My father and my bishop came to the hospital to give him a blessing; they also blessed me, promising that the righteous desires of my heart would be granted unto me. I sat in the intensive care unit waiting for my husband to come out of the coma. I had lots of time to think. I prayed constantly. I talked to the Lord about Robert. I wanted so much for him to be well. Each time I began to pray, the words of the blessing I had received came strongly into my mind—the righteous desires of my heart would be granted. I wondered what could be more righteous than to have my husband live? My young children and I needed him! I was confident that my desire was righteous.

The long days passed. I continued to ponder and struggled to understand the righteous desires of my own heart. I finally realized that what I really wanted more than anything else was the greatest possible spiritual development for my husband, my three children, and for me. After that, if God could consider the cries of my heart and let my beloved live a little longer, I would be so grateful; but I realized that the spiritual well-being of those I love was more important than whether my husband lived or died. A rush of the Spirit flowed through me and over me, assuring me that my righteous desires were also God's desires for me; we wanted the same thing. I was overwhelmed—God wanted the same thing I did. I went into that week wanting my husband to live at all costs, believing I had the faith for him to be healed. By the end of the week, I was humbled and grateful for the knowledge that whatever was needed to bring about the greatest spiritual well-being in my family was what I desired most and what God wanted too and would do. I was beginning to look at my personal struggles the same way God looked at them. In that moment, at least in that one thing, God and I were of one mind. . . .

In the world you and I will have tribulations, but Christ has overcome the world. His ways are not the ways of the world. If we truly seek to understand, our trials open the way for Christ to teach us. . . . Trials bring sorrow, which urges us to seek answers, which in turn bring understanding and peace. This is the peace which passeth the world's understanding.

Slightly modified from "The Peace Which Passeth Understanding," in Anderson, Dalton, and Green, *Every Good Thing*, 129–30.

God . . . is a shield unto them that put their trust in him.

PROVERBS 30:5

"DON'T GO INTO TIMES SQUARE!"
ALDEN PERKES

In the early 1980s I made my first trip to New York City. I would be in the city for only twenty-four hours, but I was prepared for a great adventure. I had grown up in Idaho—and I expected New York to be just a little bit different from what I was accustomed to.

I arrived mid-evening and took a cab to my hotel. In the morning I took another cab to a business meeting, which lasted until about 11 A.M. After the meeting I had my time all planned out. I didn't have any money to spare for touring, and I had only a little more time than money—I would have to leave the city to go to the airport at 4:30 in the afternoon. But given my limitations, I wanted to make the most of the experience.

If I knew then what I know now, I would have taken a different approach to the city. I probably would have gone to the Metropolitan Museum of Art and spent my entire afternoon there; or I would have spent money I didn't have to enjoy a richer experience. I might have even arranged to stay an extra day or two to take in a Broadway show and see the Statue of Liberty.

But with my limited time and funds I decided to take a walking tour of New York City. I went to the world's largest toy store (this was in December, a perfect time for a toy store!). I went into a couple of wonderful used bookstores with all sorts of nooks and crannies. I stopped at a deli and bought a pastrami on rye. And I simply wandered, my neck craned to enable me to see the tall buildings.

My plan was to walk as far as Times Square, spend some time there, and then walk back to my hotel, directly across from Central Park, where I had left my bags. The trek to Times Square covered three or four miles. When I reached the edge of the square, I was prepared to make a circuit around it, seeing the sights as I went. But the Spirit stopped me short. "Don't go into Times Square," the still small voice whispered.

I don't know what I was expecting to see at the Square. I simply knew that it was the most famous square in one of the most famous cities in the world. What I did see shocked me: porno theaters and sex shops mingled with more respectable places of business. I learned later that it was a place of high crime and low morals. (The city has since cleaned the moral squalor out of Times Square.)

The voice of the Spirit was clear, and I didn't wait to be instructed more than once. I turned and walked quickly away. It didn't matter that I had walked miles to get there. What I had found was not something I wanted.

I don't know what would have happened if I had not heeded the warning of the Spirit that day. I think of Harold B. Lee, who as a boy was prompted to stay out of a barn. He obeyed, and never did learn what the physical or spiritual danger might have been. Of course, the potential danger for me was much more obvious. As I had learned when I arrived at Times Square, much of it had been taken over by people whose very business was tempting others morally.

I'm grateful to my Father in Heaven for clearly warning me to stay out of harm's way. The danger may have been obvious, but without the warning I could well have gone into the Square "just to take a look." And in my innocent curiosity I may have unknowingly taken that first step in a direction that could have resulted in physical injury or spiritual downfall.

Instead the Lord said, in essence, "Don't even take one more step. Now turn around and get away from here." I'm grateful he spoke to me that day. And I'm grateful I heard him.

I the Lord thy God will hold thy right hand,
saying unto thee, Fear not; I will help thee.

ISAIAH 41:13

ONLY GOD GIVES A'S
BRETT G. LONDON

An institute instructor once told me that college students generally receive higher grades after completing a mission. I believed him. But that was before my mission—before I returned to college and attended an English class.

Since I was an English major, the most important class of the semester was "Analysis of Literary Forms." I needed straight A's in the final three years of college in order to be accepted by a law school I hoped to attend. Unfortunately, the professor of the class was on a personal crusade to combat grade inflation.

Adding to my anxiety was the professor's anti-religious cynicism. On the first day of class he boasted that his greatest accomplishment had been flunking a member of a religious order for cheating. Before long, I realized that I was the only Mormon in a class full of agnostics.

Our first assignment was an analysis of a short story. I spent two weeks brainstorming, outlining, writing, and rewriting until I felt assured of an A. When my paper was returned, I was sickened to see the grade was a C.

I approached the professor after class and asked what was required in order to receive an A. He responded with a sneer, "Only God gives A's." Seeing that I wasn't amused, he explained that he would award an A only if he felt the paper was worthy of publication. My grade on the next assignment was critical. This time we had only one week in which to analyze a novel, and the professor couldn't have picked a worse week. Monday night was a special family home evening. I spent Tuesday night completing my home teaching. On Wednesday, I was assigned to conduct a Young Adult activity. Thursday was quarterly stake priesthood meeting, and I had been asked to speak. On Friday I showed a friend from the mission field the sights of southern California. Saturday, I did yard work for an incapacitated family. That evening, I attended a baptism and confirmation of a close friend.

I had done absolutely nothing on the paper when Sunday arrived. The paper was due Monday morning. Since it was fast Sunday, I had no commitments that afternoon or evening. I was tempted to do my homework, rationalizing that I had been doing the Lord's work the rest of the week. This was a good example of the ox in the mire, I thought. Then I remembered that I had promised Heavenly Father that I would never do schoolwork on the Sabbath. Since I had made that personal promise to the Lord, I called upon him for strength to keep my promise.

When I awakened Monday morning, only a couple of hours remained until the deadline. I spent half of the time brainstorming and the other half typing a single draft. I had no time for an outline, revision, or corrections.

I handed in the essay, fully expecting to fail the assignment. But I had done the best I could do and still keep my promise to the Lord.

When I entered class a week later, the essays were stacked on the professor's desk. As usual, he waited until the end of class to return them. This time I was willing to wait, especially since I had no desire ever to see my paper again.

The class came to a close. The professor picked up the papers. Instead of hurriedly passing them down the rows, he just stood there, looking down at the stack. Then he began flipping through the pages of the paper on top. He slowly lifted his eyes to look at the class, hesitated for a moment and said softly, "Class, I suppose I have a reputation for being a hard grader. Well, I want you to know that today, for the first time in my teaching career, I have awarded a student an A-plus." It was my paper.

Perhaps the professor was right after all when he said, "Only God gives A's."

"Only God Gives A's." Brett G. London. Previously published in the *Ensign*, March 1988, 55–56. © by Intellectual Reserve, Inc. Used by permission.

The Spirit of the Lord Omnipotent, . . . has wrought a mighty change in us, or in our hearts, that we have no more disposition to do evil, but to do good continually.

MOSIAH 5:2

NOTHING SEEMED TO HELP
TRACEY GRIFFIN

When I was growing up I always felt I was pretty easygoing. I didn't get upset easily, and hardly ever fought with my siblings. But after my marriage I found myself becoming moody and temperamental. I'd often be emotionally on edge and would yell at my husband and children. I didn't like being that way, but I couldn't figure out how to be different.

I decided to put notes around the house to remind myself to watch my tone of voice. I determined to take a deep breath and count to ten when I found myself getting upset. Nothing seemed to help. It was easy to know the right way to act, but much harder to change my feelings.

One day I had a long talk with my dad. He had had a bad temper when I was growing up, but then had been able to overcome it. He told me he had also tried different things to change, and that nothing had worked for him either. Then he bore testimony to me that he was finally able to change with the help of the Lord.

I began to plead with great earnestness that the Lord would also help me to change in this challenging area of my life. As I pleaded sincerely and repeatedly, with full purpose of heart, he began to change my heart. He helped me to not feel so frustrated and tense about noisy kids, a messy house, or just the thousand things in a day that don't go the way you want them to.

The process took several months. Within the first week or two I began to do better from time to time, but then I would slip back. But after about four months an emotional steadiness became the norm in my life.

I still need the help of the Lord to do well. If I start to think I don't need his help anymore, I suddenly find myself slipping back into old patterns. I seek his help regularly so I can be more patient and loving, and so I can react better to my children. As I seek his help, he sends it. That has made all the difference in my life.

I STEPPED OFF THE BRIDGE
ATWELL J. PARRY

Several years ago, I went on a week-long elk hunt with two good priesthood holders from our ward. We were going into the high mountains of Idaho into the wilderness area. Because the drive took so long, we left home at 1 A.M., pulling a horse trailer with a pickup truck. We drove all day, stopping only for meals and to let the horses out to rest. It was almost dark by the time we arrived and had unloaded the pickup. We still had several miles to hike, leading our horses. We held a little council and debated whether to hike down the trail in the dark or to wait until morning. One of our group had traveled the trail before. He said that the trail was maintained by the forest service and was easy to follow even in the dark. He thought we would be able to make it to our camp by midnight. The camp was already set up; others had arrived there before us, so we wouldn't have to pitch tents in the dark.

We decided to move on. We packed all the gear on the three horses and started down the trail, each of us leading a horse and traveling single file. I was in the middle. There was just enough moonlight for us to follow the trail without using our flashlights.

The horse I was leading kept trying to hang back, and I had to keep a tight hold on his halter rope. At times it seemed like I was actually pulling him along. The man behind me could see that I was having a hard time with my reluctant horse. Without any warning, he hit the horse with a leather strap and shouted, "Get up there!" The horse bolted forward and rose up on his hind legs. When I saw the horse lunging toward me I quickly stepped to the side of the trail. What we didn't know was that we were on a forest service bridge, with no sides, over a small mountain stream. Instead of stepping to the side of the trail, I stepped off the bridge and fell six feet down into the creek.

I was still gripping the halter rope when I fell, and as a result I pulled the horse off the bridge right on top of me. He landed on his back, pushing me face down into the water, which was about a foot deep. I could feel the sand being washed out of the creek bed under me. I was able to get my head out of the water. Then the horse rolled to his side and regained his feet. As he lunged to get up the steep bank, he kicked me in the head with one of his hind hooves. I may have momentarily lost consciousness, but I'm not sure.

My two hunting buddies were not aware that I had been kicked. I finally made my way back up to the trail and told them what had happened. They couldn't see any cuts or abrasions on my head. I said I was okay. We walked some twenty minutes and then I began to go into shock. I felt like I was falling apart. I was wet and cold. My head hurt terribly, and I began to shake all over. I said, "Guys, I need to rest." I sat down on a stump and asked them to give me a blessing. We had no oil, but they laid their hands on my head and gave me a blessing. I don't remember what was said, but in a few minutes I felt better. I stopped shaking and felt good enough to walk on into camp.

As soon as we hit camp, the other men took care of my horse, put my sleeping bag in the tent, and tucked me in for the night. The next morning when I awoke I could hear them talking about the accident and wondering if they needed to take me home so I could see a doctor. I walked out of the tent and told them I felt fine. They observed that there was the clear imprint of half a horseshoe on the side of my head. I had no cuts or abrasions. I stayed the remainder of the week and felt well the entire time.

I'm grateful to know that the Lord protected me when the horse was on me in that creek, and that he healed me on the trail. Only weeks after arriving home I was called to a responsible leadership position in the Church. Because of the Lord's blessing I was alive and healthy, able to serve him according to his call.

Give, and it shall be given unto you; good measure, pressed down, and shaken together, and running over. . . . For with the same measure that ye mete withal it shall be measured to you again.

LUKE 6:38

ALL I HAD PRAYED FOR
JoAnn Taylor

Choice blessings have come to me as a direct result of my weak efforts to be obedient to the principles of the gospel, and of daily sacrifices that we all make as we try to do our best at being good parents. Wherever you have obedience you find sacrifice. They go together. I have gained a strong personal testimony of these principles over the years.

During the late 1960s and early 1970s our family had many opportunities to experience obedience and sacrifice at work. We were involved in the Indian Placement Program of the Church and had through that program met many family members on the reservation as we traveled to New Mexico each fall to bring Indian students to the Salt Lake area for schooling.

One young Navajo mother I remember well. She had come to the Salt Lake area to find work. We had many opportunities to sacrifice for her as she set up housekeeping in a small apartment close to our home.

She had many needs and would come to my door requesting food and other things for herself and her children. I thought often about the teachings of King Benjamin: "Ye yourselves will succor those that stand in need of your succor; ye will administer of your substance unto him that standeth in need; and ye will not suffer that the beggar putteth up his petition to you in vain, . . . for behold, are we not all beggars?" (Mosiah 4:16, 19).

A few days before the end of the month, and a few days after the end of the money, this struggling mother came to my door asking for bread. I went to my freezer and was surprised to find only one loaf there. Though my personal supplies were low, I knew what King Benjamin would have done, so I gave her the bread. As she walked away, I prayed to my Father in Heaven that he would help me feed my own family for the following week.

About an hour later, my telephone rang. It was a ward member whose son worked in a local bakery.

"Do you know someone who could use some bread?" she asked me. "My son brings home the extra bread at the end of the day, and my freezer's full."

I assured her that I did know someone who could use the bread. At the end of the day she arrived at my door with a paper sack full of bread and doughnuts. Each night for several weeks the same package was delivered to my doorstep—bread and sweetbreads for my family and for the Indian family as well. My freezer was full when she called me one day saying that the bakery was giving their extra bread to a service organization in the future and there would not be any more bread. I didn't mind. Heaven had poured out a blessing that I barely had room to receive.

One day our Indian friend came to my home needing furniture for her apartment, and my husband and I found what she needed in our home. As my furniture walked out the front door, I stood in the doorway of my kitchen and looked at the drapes on my front-room windows. They were threadbare. "Father in Heaven," I said in my mind, "I really need some new drapes for my front room." At the time I knew we did not have the finances to buy drapes, but I wanted them very much. There came into my mind the assurance that I would have the drapes.

A few days later I received a phone call from my brother-in-law, who had decided to remodel his home in Los Angeles. "Could you use some floor-length drapes?" he wanted to know.

"Yes," I told him. "I would love to have them."

When the drapes arrived they were a perfect fit for the two windows in my front room. I did not even have to hem them up. And inside the box with the drapes I found curtains for other areas of my house as well. It was all I had prayed for—and more.

And now, verily I say unto you, and what I say unto one I say unto all, be of good cheer, little children; for I am in your midst, and I have not forsaken you.

D&C 61:36

KEYS TO PEACE
TAMARA JOLIE

This has been an incredibly hard year for me. First I lost my father in a car accident. Eight months later I lost my mother to breast cancer. I had been home from my mother's funeral for less than a week when a good friend took her own life. Then our oldest son left on his mission. Then Tammy, our oldest daughter, had her first baby, Alison, who had serious complications. Tammy had to stay up with her night after night, getting little sleep for days on end. Finally she said, "Mom, can I leave Alison with you for a while? I'm so tired." I said, "Of course."

Shortly after Tammy left, Alison stopped breathing momentarily. I almost panicked. Then she did it again. Each time she started breathing again after a moment, but I was frantic. I tried to reach my husband, Alan, who was at work, and then Tammy, but I couldn't get either. Tammy's husband, Rick, was out of town and wouldn't be back until later that evening.

I was getting ready to call my doctor when Tammy came back

and we took Alison to the hospital. The doctor did some tests and concluded that she would require extensive heart surgery. He said as gently as he could that Alison was so weak that the chances of her survival were slim.

That night I stood for several hours and watched through the nursery window as Tammy stood in the nursery with her hands in the baby's isolette, touching the baby's head very softly. She seemed to be coaxing it with her eyes. "Don't go. Don't go."

A few minutes later we sat together—I had my arm around her and she had her head on my shoulder. I could feel Tammy's love for her little baby. Together we yearned for Heavenly Father to let us keep her.

Alan and Rick gave Alison a blessing. As I write this, Alison has survived the surgery, but she is still in intensive care. We've continued to pray. We don't know how it all will turn out, but we have faith that Heavenly Father will turn it to our good.

Such experiences are a hard way to learn. But through it all I have felt the comforting assurance from the Spirit that we will all be together again, if we remain worthy. I have been comforted to know that the Lord is near, ready and willing to bless and strengthen us in our trials. And through these terribly challenging experiences the Lord has finally helped me to understand what it really means to *love* a member of your family with a deep, eternal, yearning, longing love. I'm not sure I would have gained that priceless understanding in any other way.

Let thy bowels also be full of charity towards all men.

D&C 121:45

THE LORD'S GIFT OF LOVE
DANIEL A. TOLMAN

I'm not sure why, but I grew up feeling quite judgmental and critical of other people. I would see a panhandler on the street and would wonder why he didn't get a job. If an unkempt man or woman got onto the transit bus, I would mentally criticize them for not taking better care of themselves. When I saw someone on the TV news who had suffered a tragic loss of home or property and was broken up about it, I would mentally ask them why they placed so much value on temporal things.

When I was dealing with friends and family I was thoughtful and caring (at least that was my personal view of myself). But when I looked at people I didn't know, I would judge them, whether positively or negatively, and my judgment would often be harsh and unloving. To make matters worse, all of this judgment and lack of love was subconscious; I wasn't even aware that I was doing it.

I knew the Lord's commandment that I must love my neighbor as myself. I knew that loving my neighbor (even panhandling, unkempt "Samaritans") was the second greatest commandment. And certainly I treated everyone with respect. But somehow that knowledge hadn't reached the feeling level of my heart.

As I grew and progressed in the gospel, I went through a series of stages, as I suppose everyone does. First I knew that I needed to overcome a number of weaknesses if I wanted to please God. Then, having done well in that effort over time and continuing in faithfulness, I felt I was safely on track. But finally, I had a feeling of "divine discontent" (as Elder Neal A. Maxwell puts it), and with the help of the Lord I was able to identify other areas of my life where I fell short. One serious flaw the Lord showed me was my lack of a loving and compassionate heart.

I began to pray for the gift of charity. Over time I felt my feelings soften some, but I knew I still had a long way to go.

"What more can I do?" I asked. It wasn't my behavior that I was trying to change; it was my heart. One day I saw a young man get on the bus with a companion and sit only a few seats away from me. He had several earrings in each ear. He had long, straggly, blond hair; it looked like it hadn't been washed for weeks. His jeans were torn and his sandled feet were dirty. He carried the smell of alcohol about him. He and his companion were talking loudly enough that I could hear their coarse, vulgar language. As I began to slip into my old mode of being judgmental, I stopped myself and begged the Lord for forgiveness. "How could I judge one of thy children like that?" I asked. "Judging is wrong. I don't even know the man."

While I was praying in my heart, the Spirit whispered, "Ask

your Father in Heaven if you can see this young man as he sees him." I was surprised at the thought, but I followed the prompting. I was almost immediately filled with a deep feeling of sadness at the course in life the young man had taken. And then, right on the heels of that first feeling, I felt a love for this man I had never met. Instead of wanting to judge him, I wanted to bless him.

Not long after that, I saw an older woman who looked like she had had a hard life. She wasn't the kind of person I would normally want to have anything to do with. "Ask your Father in Heaven if he will help you love this woman," the Spirit whispered, not in words but in a clear feeling. I silently offered a prayer asking for the gift of love for that specific woman. The feeling came instantly, filling my heart. I knew that this woman, despite any mistakes she had made in life, had true value to our Father, and that she must have value to me also. What's more, I didn't simply know it intellectually. I felt in my heart that feeling of the value of this, my sister, to our Heavenly Father and to me.

I have seldom since fallen back into the spirit of judgment. I don't like the way that spirit feels, and when my mind starts to take me there, I utter a prayer in my heart that the Lord will grant me the wonderful gift of his love. As I seek it, seeking also to be worthy and to honestly be open to the blessing, it comes and softens my life.

The prayers of the faithful shall be heard.

2 NEPHI 26:15

WE CALLED A FAMILY FAST
BRANDON R. WILLIAMS

As the time drew near for the birth of our new baby, we were told that the baby was in a breech position, and it was probably too late in the pregnancy to expect the baby to turn. The head was up and the body was down, just the opposite of a normal birth position. At this time C-sections were not as common as they are now. Our previous child had been born breech, and we knew all too well how much harder it was for the mother to give birth to a breech baby, and what complications could occur. In our deep concern we called a family fast. We hoped that, if it was the Lord's will, the baby might change position—and we also knew that my wife, Renee, needed the comfort that our prayers could bring.

During the night after the special fast and family prayer, Renee was awakened with a great commotion inside her. She described the motion as one that almost knocked her out of bed. She said it felt like the baby, who was almost due, was doing somersaults. At the next doctor's visit we discovered that the baby had indeed turned around and that the head was now in the proper position. We were relieved and very thankful.

When it came time for the delivery, even though the labor was constant and everything seemed ready, there was very little progress. It seemed to the doctor that the baby's head was not engaging. When the membranes ruptured, the doctor soon discovered that the cord was wrapped around the baby's neck, probably as a result of the somersault he had done previously. The doctor quickly moved the cord from around the baby's head, and the delivery was complete within twenty more minutes. The baby's bluish color soon turned to pink, and we had a healthy eight-and-a-half-pound boy.

Gratitude filled our hearts as we realized that in receiving one great blessing, and then another, we were able to welcome this little boy whole and healthy, a gift from a loving Heavenly Father.

Ye have heard his voice from time to time;
and he hath spoken unto you in a still small voice.

1 NEPHI 17:45

"GO INTO ANOTHER ROOM"
JOYCE LINDSTROM

I knew that the Van Hooser family had settled in Bethany, Missouri, at an early date. I met my cousin Jay Lamb in Columbia, Missouri, and from there we drove to Bethany.

In Bethany we went to the county clerk's office. [We thought] the only records in that office of genealogical value to us were birth records. While I copied the Van Hooser names from those registers, something kept saying to me, "Go into another room. Don't waste your time here."

When I had copied those records, we went into the room where the marriage and deed records were kept. As I tried to copy the Van Hooser marriages from the records, this same insistent feeling recurred—"Go to another room. Don't waste your time here." Now, as valuable as marriage records are, I couldn't understand this inner urge to quit working in these records. But finally I couldn't concentrate on the marriages, and told Jay that I was going into the probate office.

While working on the Van Hooser probates, I ran across the

probate record of Lydia Van Hooser. Reading through her records, I found her to be my Lydia Van Hooser who had lived previously in Troy, Illinois. I knew this branch of the Van Hooser family had left Troy by 1860, when the census was taken, but I didn't know where they had gone.

Now I knew. Since Lydia Van Hooser never married, she had left her property to sisters, nieces, and nephews. This is why I had to go to Bethany—to find this will and all other papers pertaining to the distribution of Lydia's estate. Once I knew this was where the Van Hooser descendants had moved, I searched the probate records regarding other surnames of interest to me, and found a wealth of genealogical information. I worked most of the day in the probate office. When I felt as though I had covered the records there, I returned to the room where the marriages were kept. I was then able to concentrate on the marriages and found a great many more pertaining to those mentioned in Lydia Van Hooser's will than I would ever have found or identified before.

Genealogy is the Lord's work and if we do all we can in behalf of our ancestors and still need more help, the aid of the Lord is always nearby. What we must do is kneel in prayer with faith and ask for divine aid.

"My Genealogical Mission," *Improvement Era*, September 1964, 766–67.

Trust in the Lord with all thine heart;
and lean not unto thine own understanding.
In all thy ways acknowledge him,
and he shall direct thy paths.

PROVERBS 3:5–6

TRUST THE PATH I WALK
DEBRA SANSING WOODS

Like many women, my plate is full—so full, sometimes, that I feel like a wagon being pulled by several teams of horses all going in different directions. My heart is genuinely engaged in rearing my three young daughters, running a home-based business as a certified public accountant and professional speaker, volunteering in our community, serving as the Young Women president in my ward, and sneaking in uninterrupted time with my husband whenever possible. Often I run so fast and hard that I feel more splintered than centered. When my pace is too fast for too long, life usually hands me an invitation to slow down, to see more clearly where I am now and where I am heading.

One Friday morning several months ago, such invitations began to arrive. While I raced to thoroughly clean the kitchen and family room, my two youngest daughters played upstairs.

Pausing to check on them, I found Samantha, my three-year-old, sitting at the top of the stairs, distressed and struggling for air. She whispered that she had swallowed something. She was getting some air, but her purplish color and wheezy, rattled gasping suggested that something was terribly wrong. I had taken CPR, but I wasn't sure whether to do the Heimlich maneuver or give her something to drink. With my adrenaline rushing and Kelly, my two-year-old, following close behind me, I carried Samantha downstairs to call 911. I didn't want to be alone if I had to fight for my daughter's life.

Speaking to the 911 dispatcher while holding Samantha, I managed to explain our crisis. The dispatcher said to do nothing except watch Samantha carefully—no Heimlich, no drink. Some air was better than no air. She was sending help. Stay as calm as possible. Samantha would take her cues from me.

While waiting for the paramedics, I looked out the window into the quiet sunny day, looking for some sign that help was really coming. I watched Samantha closely, trying to soothe her while I felt paralyzed by the fear that her breathing obstruction would become complete. Once the paramedics arrived, they quickly assessed the situation and agreed that she had swallowed something that had gone down her windpipe and now obstructed her normal breathing. Our neighbor took Kelly to her home so I could ride to the hospital in the ambulance with Samantha.

The emergency room doctor called in an ear, nose, and throat specialist to examine Samantha. The specialist explained that a bronchioscopy was needed, a procedure in which Samantha would be put under general anesthesia. They would insert a probe down her throat to look for the foreign object and attempt to remove it. Although I was nervous about the procedure and attendant risks, there wasn't a viable alternative. The procedure was completed in less than thirty minutes. The surgeon located and removed a large, blue bead blocking air from entering her right lung.

Samantha was going to be okay. The scare was over, but this experience made me think of how much I loved my daughters. My business pursuits seemed small, pale, and unimportant in comparison. I felt deep gratitude as we brought Samantha home from the hospital the next day. The ordeal had been frightening and exhausting, but we were happy to have her safely home. I looked forward to some rest and a return to our normal routine.

Still emotionally and physically drained from the bead episode, I woke Monday morning to find Samantha in our bed, hot with fever. Our family doctor ran some tests, concerned that the temperature indicated a possible infection related to the surgery. The test results showed that this was unlikely, but the doctor suggested we keep a close eye on her. We soon realized that she had the flu that had been running rampant through our community. Being up during the nights with Samantha and up during the days with my other children left me exhausted.

Wednesday morning I woke weary, desperate for some uninterrupted sleep. Kelly woke soon after me with a 103-degree fever. Samantha's fever continued. My husband, under serious deadlines at work, was unable to provide any relief to the daytime demands of caring for our sick children. I didn't ask others to help because I didn't want to risk making them sick.

Although exhausted, I was blessed with enough energy and focus to care for my children. The previous week, before the bead episode, I had prepared and distributed the marketing materials for my upcoming money-management seminar. I felt relieved that I was ahead of schedule until I received a phone call telling me that a large part of my advertising had irretrievably fallen through, which meant fewer participants would attend my next workshop. With sick children I could do nothing to make up for this loss.

Discouraged, I sat down to nurse my toddler. While nursing, I noticed a distinct, pea-sized lump in my breast. Was it mastitis? No, this was clearly something else. My mind pored over the possibilities, dwelling on the worst. I didn't have a family history of breast cancer. Was it even possible for a nursing mother to have breast cancer? I didn't know. The phone rang. The elementary school nurse was calling to say that Amanda, my seven-year-old was running a fever. Tears surfaced as I looked down to see Kelly sleeping.

Once my sister drove Amanda home, we all rested until the girls couldn't stand being confined indoors any longer. They headed into the backyard to play—as much as three sick children can. Watching from the deck, I cried a silent prayer to Heavenly Father, earnestly asking, "What is it that you want me to learn from this past week?" The answer came immediately, simply, and unmistakably: "Trust." The Spirit confirmed this impression.

Listening to the Lord, I saw that my feet were planted in fear—the immediate fear that I might have breast cancer and that if I did have cancer, I might lose my life. If that happened, what would happen to my girls? Then I saw clearly that fear was not isolated to today or this past week; other fears tugged at my consciousness.

I feared for my family's financial future. I feared that I was not a good enough mother. I feared the disapproval of others. As hard as I tried, whatever I did never seemed good enough. I shrugged off compliments and kept track of the criticisms I had received over the years. I dealt with my fears by working harder and faster to make things better and to prove myself, only to end up feeling scattered and defeated because I could never do enough.

Now, in this crisis, Heavenly Father had clearly lit his path—the path of trust. Trust that I could focus on rearing my children without feeling driven to earn income for our future financial security. I didn't have to set the professional speaking or financial planning world on fire today. That season would come. Trust that parenting with my whole heart and my best but imperfect efforts were good enough. Trust that the blessings that my bishop and husband had given me—telling me how pleased the Lord was with my efforts—were true. Trust that I could handle whatever challenges came into my life. Trust that if something were to happen to me, my daughters would be taken care of.

Choosing trust was such a welcome change. It brought the attending gifts of comfort, peace, hope, and confidence. Things began to look up. My doctor determined that the breast lump was a benign cyst. My children were healthy again. We were meeting our financial challenges with faith and hope. I came down with the flu, but I used the time in bed to rest and ponder the lessons of the past week.

Learning to trust is an active process for me. When I find myself overwhelmed by worry or fear, I pause to pray for peace and clarity. With the help of the Spirit, I determine if there is some action I should take to address the source of the fear. I earnestly search the scriptures for answers and comfort. Two of my favorite scriptures are Proverbs 3:5–6, "Trust in the Lord with all thine heart; and lean not unto thine own understanding. In all thy ways acknowledge him, and he shall direct thy paths," and 2 Timothy 1:7, "For God hath not given us the spirit of fear; but of power, and of love, and of a sound mind." When I do my part and trust in Heavenly Father's plan for me, I feel less rushed, less burdened, and more capable. I see with clearer vision his path, the path to eternal life.

Thy Word Is a Lamp: Women's Stories of Finding Light, 129–33.

I the Lord thy God will hold thy right hand,
saying unto thee, Fear not; I will help thee.

ISAIAH 41:13

IT SOLD ON THE LAST DAY
THOMAS R. CLARK

A few years ago a developer began to subdivide a large parcel of land just west of our home. The newly divided property had two building lots that joined our backyard. We were hoping that some of our children could purchase the property and build their own houses next to ours, but none were in a financial position to do so.

In time, the lots began to be filled with new construction, and houses were in various stages of completion. Soon the only building lot that had no construction on it was the one that most completely joined our property.

As we considered the matter spiritually, we felt we ought to make an inquiry concerning its status. Since no construction was evident, we thought maybe it had not been purchased. But we were informed that the whole development had been sold out for more than two years. We asked the developer to call us if anything changed, making the lot next to us available.

Three months later we still hadn't heard anything and felt

impressed that we should call again. This time we learned that the young couple owning the lot had had some unexpected medical expenses and had decided to sell the lot.

In the meantime, our oldest son, Paul, had experienced increasing financial success. He was aware of the lot next to ours and began to feel some stirrings of the Spirit that he could purchase that lot if he could sell his existing home. With the blessing of his wife, Sheryl, he paid some earnest money on the property and put their home up for sale. They had three months to close on the lot before losing their earnest money and the property.

Two months and three weeks went by and their home still hadn't sold. We were growing increasingly concerned. The housing market had been cycling downward for quite some time and things didn't look very promising. But when Paul and Sheryl prayed about it, they still felt a reassurance that the move was right and that somehow their house would be sold in time. In that final week, the real estate agent recommended that they reduce the price on their home to encourage a quicker sale, but that would leave them with too little money to build their new house. Again Paul and Sheryl prayed, and they felt they should stand firm on the asking price. They felt that for some reason the Lord was motivating them to make this move, and that he would open doors to make it possible.

Within two days they had an offer on their house at full price; just a few days later, on the very last day of eligibility for the earnest money agreement, they were able to close the sale on both their house and the purchase of the lot adjoining ours.

They have since built a fine new home with a backyard adjacent to ours, making a nice big area for play and gardening. We enjoy a wonderful relationship with Paul and his family and are very grateful that the Lord helped both in giving guidance and in opening the way for a move that is proving to be a blessing to their entire family.

O God, . . . thou wast merciful unto me when I did cry unto thee . . . ; when I did cry unto thee in my prayer, . . . thou didst hear me.

THE GAS GAUGE WAS BELOW EMPTY
JENNA LEE

I am a single mom with six children. My six-year-old son had just celebrated a birthday and was now seven. We wanted to do something special for his birthday but I had very little money. I had some tickets that I had previously purchased to see *Beauty and the Beast* at the Capitol Theater and felt that this would be just the experience to share with my son.

The day came and I was frantically trying to feed all my children and get them ready for bed so I could leave. When it was time to leave I was running behind schedule. I didn't feel like I could afford to spend the money to park near the theater, but because I was late I grabbed the money I had—six dollars—and headed for town.

We hadn't traveled far when I noticed that the gas gauge was below empty. I knew if I stopped for gas we'd be late for the show, and the ushers wouldn't seat us until there was a break. As I drove I prayed for guidance. Should I stop and get gas—and be late? Or take my chances that we wouldn't run out of gas and that we'd be on time for the play? A quiet feeling came that I should continue driving and that my son and I would make it to our destination.

But I still worried. What if I had misunderstood that quiet impression? Maybe I should stop and put one dollar's worth of gas in the car. Then I might still have enough to pay for parking. Or I could use all of the money for gas and find a more distant parking place, where I could park for free. But as I pondered my options, I still felt like I should just drive to the theater.

Then, as I neared town, an image of a certain parking lot came to my mind. It was just across the street from the Capitol Theater, and my memory said that it was a little cheaper than the parking garage adjacent to the theater. I asked in prayer if the impression that I should park in that particular lot had come from the Lord, and I felt it had. Logically it didn't make a lot of sense. But I knew I would save one dollar by parking there, and maybe that was reason enough.

When I arrived in town I parked across the street from the theater in the place that had been brought to my mind. We jumped out of the car and barely made it on time to see the show. My son was thrilled with the production; it was a blessing for both of us to be able to share that special time together.

When the play was over, we went back to the car and waited in a long line to get out of the parking lot; all the while I was fearful that we might run out of gas before we even made it out of the lot. My heart was filled with gratitude that we had made it that far, and I prayed that, if it was the Lord's will, we'd be able to make it to a gas station. As I prayed, I received a warm reassurance that we would be all right.

When we finally rounded the corner so that I could see the booth, the man taking the money started waving everyone out of the lot. We left the parking lot without having to pay a dime.

With guidance, we found a gas station that was both near and open and I was able to put all six dollars worth of gas into my car.

What a blessing! Small and relatively unimportant, perhaps—but I cannot deny the help Heavenly Father gave me that day.

The Lord preserveth all them that love him.

PSALM 145:20

A PRAYER ON THE RUN
JON M. TAYLOR

I was sixteen years of age when my father, my older brother, and I traveled to Yellowstone Park to see its sights for the first time. We camped for the night in a tent at Fishing Bridge, near the Yellowstone River. We had taken some fishing gear and were going to rise early to fish at the side of the river.

About 4:30 A.M., the alarm went off, but my father and brother were too tired to get up, even with repeated efforts to awaken them. So I decided to go on my own. I grabbed my pole and fishing gear and headed down a trail towards the river. By this time, daylight was just beginning to break through the trees in the forest, but it was still somewhat dark

Soon a series of booming sounds echoed through the forest. The sound reminded me of a woodsman cutting down a tree with a long-handled axe. But this sound kept growing louder and louder until I realized that, whatever it was, it was getting closer and closer to me!

As I turned in the direction of the sound I saw a huge bear heading straight toward me. The sound was its enormous paws hitting the forest floor—"Boom . . . Boom . . . BOOM . . . BOOM!"

I turned and walked away from the bear. It followed me. I tried to change directions, to hide, to dodge around trees—but it kept right after me. The thought of climbing a tree crossed my mind, but I was not sure the bear would give me time to do so. I became less and less hopeful of evading him in the forest. After all, this was the bear's territory—not mine. I began calling out for help. While trying to evade the bear, I knocked and shook the doors of parked campers, but they were all locked. All the while, the bear kept coming.

Finally, in desperation I decided to pray. Normally, I would find a secluded place and kneel down where I could concentrate on my communion with the Lord. But to keep moving seemed a wiser decision. I prayed with all my heart as I stumbled through the forest, the bear in hot pursuit. "Dear Father, what should I do? Please show me NOW!"

Immediately a scene came into my mind—an animal trainer at a circus I had seen. I asked myself, "When the bears or big cats became unruly, what did the trainer do?" I remembered that the trainer would aim something directly at the eyes of the animal, and it would back off.

But what did I have to ward off this big bear? My fishing pole!

I stopped abruptly, spun around 180 degrees, and faced the bear with the fishing pole pointed right at its snout. It stopped, weaving its head back and forth, seemingly bewildered by my action. The bear backed off and began to retreat from me—then wheeled around and again came toward me.

I held my position, extending the fishing pole in the direction of its eyes. My arm was shaking so badly the fishing pole could have appeared to be anything to the bear. Finally, that powerful bundle of muscle and fur stopped, turned, and headed back into the forest.

Suddenly, I could hear the opening of camper doors (that had before been locked) and people calling out, "Was that a bear?" "Are you all right?"

The next morning I told the park ranger about my experience. He told me I was very fortunate—that only a few months before, a man had been killed by a bear under almost identical circumstances.

I thanked the Lord for answering my prayer on the run.

He giveth power to the faint; and to them
that have no might he increaseth strength. . . .
But they that wait upon the Lord shall
renew their strength; . . . they shall run, and
not be weary; and they shall walk, and not faint.

ISAIAH 40:29, 31

THE ROAD BACK HOME
MARGARET BARTON WILSON

In the summer of 1972 our fourth child, Lynda Margaret, arrived on my birthday, June 3. Just a month later, on fast Sunday, July 2, we rejoiced at both the blessing of our new baby and the confirmation of our firstborn son, Bart. But sorrow overcame me when we returned home from church and received news of the death of my beloved maternal grandmother, Margaret Elizabeth Eldredge. Grandma and Grandpa Eldredge were always a near-perfect example to me of righteousness and happiness. We had grown up very close to them because of their great capacity to love and serve. Facing life without her was very hard for me to bear.

After the funeral I felt deep loneliness and sorrow. As the days passed, a yearning to go home to visit my parents started to build within me. Because of his heavy summer responsibilities on our farm, it was impossible for my husband, Cliff, to take me. Then one day, as if in answer to prayer, my sister Linda phoned me. She had been having similar feelings about going home, and offered to make the drive with me.

For us, "home" is the wide-open spaces of a cattle ranch called the Diamond A, located on the border of southwestern Idaho and northern Nevada between the Jarbidge and Bruneau rivers. It is nestled along Buck Creek in a canyon quite isolated and yet easily accessible. The ranch is about a hundred miles from Nampa, Idaho, "as the crow flies," but about two hundred and fifty miles if one takes the good roads going in from the Twin Falls side. We planned to take the shortcut across the Bruneau desert. To cross the desert we would travel fifty miles to Bruneau, go across the southeastern edge of the Mountain Home Air Force Base bombing range, then take eighty miles of dirt roads to intersect with the road that comes in from the Twin Falls side. Because there are no telephones at the ranch we could not call to tell our parents of our plans, but we did send word by way of our friends, the Smacks, from Twin Falls.

We left at 7 A.M. on August 2. We took a bunch of bananas and a thermos of water, along with some Gerber's cottage cheese and mashed bananas for the baby. We fully expected to be at the ranch in several hours and knew breakfast would be waiting for us. We hoped it would be brook trout from the creek and hash-browns. Linda was driving her yellow Mercury Cougar; I sat in the passenger seat holding the baby, and my three other children (Bart, Craig, and Angie) rode in the back.

The children had eaten the bananas and consumed half of the water before we even reached the little town of Bruneau. By this time we were beyond the bombing range and had started across a vast area with very little habitation.

As we drove down the dirt road, we started running into ruts from heavy trucks that had made many trips hauling water to the cattle. In time the ruts got deeper and harder to get through. My heart raced at the thought of getting stuck. The dirt that filled the ruts was a fine, dry, powdery dust that was slippery and consuming. The road was bumpy and it was hard to steer.

Suddenly Linda had to make a split decision to either drive between the ruts or go around them into the barrow pit. She chose to drive through, trying to keep the wheels out of the ruts. As she started through, the car wheel pulled hard, and suddenly we went down into the deep ruts. The car was high centered on the sun-baked hard pack with the wheels spinning in the powdery dirt. We couldn't move forward or back. We were both panic-stricken, with no idea what to do.

We said a short prayer and then hopped out and tried to dig out and chip away the cement-like dirt with sticks of sagebrush. When the task proved too difficult we got back in the car and prayed again for help and another idea. I knew the Lord would help us. We decided to jack up the car and fill the ruts with rocks and brush to support the wheels. It didn't work, and panic spread to deeper panic as we realized how unprepared we were. Dad had always said, "Always carry a shovel and plenty of water when you are traveling." We had neither.

It was 8:30 in the morning and the sun was already getting hot. Humbled by our lack of preparation, we got back into the car and explained to the children what our situation was. We bowed our heads and prayed a little more fervently for the Lord's help. After pondering a few minutes, we decided to pull some of the tall, dead sagebrush and put it under the wheels for traction. We had no gloves, and as we pulled at the sagebrush it scratched and cut into our skin. Our hands were soon bleeding and blistered, and we tore up diapers to make bandages. Little whirlwinds kept coming along and whipped the dust around us, and soon we were all covered with a fine layer of dirt. The children started to get thirsty and cranky—and anxious about our situation. The dust irritated our lungs and made it difficult to work under the car. Finally we managed to get sagebrush under the wheels and chipped away the hard dirt in the center underneath. We let the jack down, changed our dirty clothes, and tried to drive the car out. It didn't take more than a few tries to see that our efforts had been in vain.

Bart, Craig, and Angie were getting a little more impatient and restless with the dust and heat and hunger by now. I opened a jar of the baby food, but they didn't like it much. I let them take some sips of the small amount of water we had left, and we prayed for help once more.

We discussed our options: Clover Crossing was about ten to fifteen miles behind us, but it had appeared to be totally vacated when we passed through. We figured that Bracketts' ranch and the junction of the road from Twin Falls, which was quite frequently traveled, had to be at least twenty to thirty miles ahead of us. We wondered which way to go for help—or even if that was the right thing to do. By now it was just past noon and quite hot, so the worst of the heat was yet to come.

I was growing increasingly concerned about the children. Bart was just eight years old, but was quite calm and easygoing about most things. Craig, aged five, seemed to be the most impatient. He could see the Jarbidge Mountain in the distance and the canyons beneath it and knew the ranch was there. He had no concept of distance and wondered why we couldn't just walk over there and get Grandpa to pull us out. He seemed to blame us for his discomfort and the situation and jabbered constantly. Angie, just two years old, didn't understand anything except that she was miserable and uncomfortable, hot, hungry, and thirsty for more than her allotted sip of water. She cried only because her physical needs were not being met. The baby seemed to be doing the best of all of us. Even though her nostrils were full of dust and it was hot, she slept most of the time and was content.

We had never known such thirst, and our need for water became the most important thing. I nursed baby Lynda as needed, and wondered how long I would be able to do that without water.

Linda felt that she wanted to walk to the Bracketts. I would stay with the children and she would go for help. The water was completely gone now and there was none for her to take with her. It was very hot and I doubted that she could ever make that distance in the heat without water. She started down the road, but didn't get far before she knew by the Spirit that that was the wrong thing to do. She turned back and again we prayed, even more fervently, for guidance.

We scanned the desert behind us and in the distance we could see a canyon and what appeared to be a haystack. We could see fresh cow pies and a cattle trail that certainly led to water. Being raised on a ranch, we knew that most ranches have "winter camps" out on the range, usually with a cabin and corrals for their horses and a haystack nearby. We knew there would probably be water there and maybe some food. Linda decided she could take Bart and hike down to it (probably about five miles) to find what she could. With his little pioneering Cub Scout spirit, Bart was eager to be a "helper" and was keen about going along.

They set out about 2 P.M. I watched them until they were out of sight. Emotions were close to the surface as I saw them disappear and wondered what would happen. I sensed my lack of faith and prayed many times that afternoon. Whirlwinds continued to rise up and fool me into thinking help was coming, but the clouds of dust went away as fast as they appeared.

Angie cried and cried and became more dehydrated as the afternoon passed. The baby slept, and Craig was enraged at his mother for not walking over there to get Grandpa. Our failure to get out decreased his faith in our abilities, but he continued to pray with me and never seemed to doubt that his Heavenly Father would help us if I would only cooperate.

I began to worry as the hours passed and six o'clock came and went and they hadn't returned. I prayed and pondered over what we might do when they returned. I decided I should walk south to the Bracketts' ranch for help. The temperature would cool down, and with some water I could make it. I asked Heavenly Father if that was indeed the right course to take, and right away I received a confirmation of the Spirit that it was. I put on the warmest clothes I had with me and changed from my sandals into an old pair of shoes I had brought to fish in. I began to psych myself up for walking that far. How I wished I were better prepared physically. Having given birth to a baby only two months before, I felt very inadequate. But the Spirit waxed strong, and I began to feel extra reservoirs of physical strength, as well as spiritual. I knew it was right and the Lord would help deliver us from our plight.

At about 7:30 I walked to a rise in the road and could see two specks coming toward us. Soon the hues of red in Bart's shirt brought relief to my tired eyes. How grateful I was for their safe return! They were carrying several old cans of water and packages of soda crackers. It was like manna from heaven to us all. Linda and Bart told us that after a couple of hours of walking, they had come upon a small cow camp that included a stuffy old abandoned cabin. There they found the soda crackers and several canteens that they had filled with water. They left a note to tell the owners what they had taken and to say thanks.

We were elated; it seemed too good to be true to the kids. We spread the blanket on the ground and ate a supper of soda crackers and water that wasn't all that pure, but we blessed it and were so grateful.

I nursed the baby and told everyone of my decision to walk for help. Craig was relieved that I was finally going to do the right thing. Linda would bed them down as best she could and, with a jar of baby food and a pacifier, would take care of the baby until I returned with help. Linda and Bart were exhausted from walking in the heat all afternoon, and I hated to leave her there with the full responsibility of my little family. But our success was in the hands of the Lord and we would rely on him. I strapped a thermos of water around my waist and tried my best to be cheerful instead of teary, kissed them all, and set out for Bracketts' ranch.

I had reached a cattle guard about a half-mile down the road when Primary songs began filling my mind and my heart. I sang every one I knew and some of my favorites twice. I was indeed strengthened by each song and sang for several hours without stopping. I seemed to recall the words as never before. Every one seemed to have a special message for me. "Pioneer children sang as they walked and walked and walked . . ." I thought of the pioneers and how this would have been a typical day's work for them. When I ran out of Primary songs and hymns, I recalled "When It's Nighttime in Nevada" and many of the old family favorites we sang around the piano while we were growing up. There was "Home on the Range" and "Our Mountain Home, So Dear," and many others.

The road looked so long ahead of me, and the sun began to drop low on the horizon. I was frightened by the bobcat tracks I had seen all over the road, but kept on singing and gathered all my courage about me. "I Am a Child of God" brought a lump to my throat and tears to my eyes, and gave me the additional strength I needed. I sang it over and over again and the fear left me. I remembered a quotation my brother, Bob, had learned on his mission to England and recited many times. It went, "There is no circumstance, no fate, no destiny that can circumvent or control the firm resolve of the determined soul." I was determined. I had set a goal, and I was determined to reach it, and there was nothing that would stop me unless it was myself. I knew the Lord was with me and I would arrive in due time.

I knew the Lord was with Linda and my children too. She later told me how it grew dark and she arranged blankets in the car for them. Soon Angie, Craig, and Bart were asleep. Linda closed her eyes, but she was too worried to sleep. "Was Peg able to follow the road in the darkness? Had a wild animal of the night attacked her? Had she fallen and was hurt with no one to help her?" The questions raced through her mind. Occasionally, sweet baby Lynda would make a noise and my sister would dip the pacifier in banana-cottage cheese baby food and pop it back into her mouth. Lynda would quiet down, but soon would repeat the routine. All night Linda could see far off in the distance the lights from cars that were traveling along the highway. They looked so far away, but they gave her assurance that there was hope. She had faith that I would find help for us.

As I plodded along, my mind raced with questions of my own. Comfort came as I thought how the desert had always been my friend. Dad had always told us that bobcats and cougars were afraid of man and would never attack unless threatened or cornered. Remembering that quieted my fears.

The air temperature was changing, and I was glad for the jacket I had tied around my waist. I kept the pace steady and stopped only to sip the water, even though I was already starting to tire. How would I make it all the way?

My thoughts turned to Grandma Eldredge once again and what she had always meant to me; the encouragement and strength she had always given me; the many things she had taught me with patience to do. When I'd visit her as a child she always had something to share with me or a project for us to accomplish. She would work right alongside me until it was completed. I loved to wash her dishes, because she'd always dry them and we'd talk about wonderful things. She had always exhibited faith in me and in my abilities to accomplish what I set out to do.

But oh, I was growing weary of walking! The recollections of Grandma's example gave me renewed determination to keep going. I took another sip of water and then Grandma's voice came into my mind just as if she were walking along with me. She was telling me she knew I could make it. I could feel her presence with me, and I wept. It gave me another glimpse of heaven to feel her so close and to know that she knew what I was doing and had faith in me still.

The sky was full of brilliant stars. I pondered for a time on the size of the universe, all those stars, and the worlds without end the Lord had created. I wondered how he could be so mindful of me, one young woman, stranded in the desert. But I knew beyond doubt that he was, and I could feel the Spirit guiding me and urging me onward. Much of my testimony was born that night as I contemplated my relationship with my Father and his Son, Jesus Christ—my light and my strength. How I loved him for the sacrifice he made for us all—and for the personal love and concern he was showing me that night.

The stars seemed to move across the sky, and I wondered what time it was. I was so tired and my hips ached. I could feel the blisters on my feet and wanted to lie down just for a minute, but I didn't dare for fear I'd go to sleep. I had to keep plodding along, no matter how uncomfortable and tired I became.

The air was quite cold now, and I could feel the air temperature change continually as I walked and climbed to a higher plateau of the desert. Even though it was chilly, I was so exhausted that I decided to rest just for a moment, in spite of my fear of going to sleep for several hours. I lay down on the road; it felt so good to relax. My hips and feet and legs throbbed as my eyes closed. I did go to sleep, but I woke up running down the road chilled and shivering. It was as if someone had picked me up and sent me on my way. When I was fully awake I slowed the pace and felt grateful for the assistance the Lord had given me in my weakness.

I knew I had to exercise all the self-discipline I was capable of to keep walking and not give in to the signals my body was sending to my brain to sleep and rest. I prayed once again for strength and realized my growing doubt and discouragement was a result of my weariness and lack of confidence. All that kept me going was the love I felt for my children and sister. Then I thought of the saying, "It always seems darkest before the dawn."

The stars continued to move farther across the sky, and before long I saw the first glimpse of daylight over the horizon. I made out the image of a horse grazing not far from the road. My hips were so stiff I could hardly put one foot in front of the other.

As I came up over the rise, I could see the power lines in the distance and felt a thrill of excitement to know where I was and that I didn't have far to go.

Remembering my family miles behind me helped me quicken my step in spite of the pain. Every step was an effort, but I struggled onward. The goal was in sight and the pain just a constant reminder of the determination I needed.

At last I looked down over the ridge at the Bracketts' home. The meadows had never looked so pretty, even though they had turned yellow in the August heat. The sun was barely ready to come over the horizon as I left the road to take a shortcut over the side of the hill, cutting off a mile or two.

It was 6:30 A.M. and it had taken me ten hours, but I was nearly there. The thought of getting someone to go out after my family warmed my heart and I felt another glimpse of joy. The Lord had indeed answered my prayer, even though he had required of me a true sacrifice to use all my faculties and to keep my feet moving every step. He was the source of strength and inspiration I had needed to meet the challenge.

I knocked at the Bracketts' door with tears of relief and

gratitude streaming down my face, mixing with the layers of dust that had built up over the last twenty-two hours. No one answered and I knocked louder and longer, thinking maybe they weren't yet awake. Still there was no response. I walked to the hired hand's house about fifty yards away. I didn't linger there long when there was no answer.

The Bracketts' son, Bert, lived down the road a mile or so, and I didn't relish the thought of having to walk that much farther. Then I noticed a trailer house behind some willows near the house, with a car parked beside it. I knocked on the door. When it opened, the relief I felt was overwhelming. The trailer was occupied by a man and his wife who had taken a job there several days before. It was hard to get the words out, and my voice broke as I told them of my predicament. They gave me a drink of water and immediately took me up the road to Bert's house.

Bert and Paula and their family were just sitting down to breakfast. He was surprised to see me, especially in the condition I was in. I will never forget their kindness and empathy towards me as they saw my total exhaustion and concern for my family. They invited me to eat with them, but I couldn't waste a moment to rescue my family. Paula immediately packed all the food on their table to take with us, and we started out in Bert's pickup. I told him I thought it was about twenty miles out; he took note of his speedometer in order to check the distance. When we had gone twenty miles there was still no sign of the car. After twelve more miles we arrived on the scene of the car and Linda and the children. Twenty-four hours had passed since we had gotten stuck.

We found them tired and hungry, under layers of dust. My baby had dried baby food all over her face. Linda and the children hugged me tightly. The car was covered with dust that was literally an inch high. Bert spread the breakfast over the hood of the truck; orange juice and cantaloupe had never tasted so good. Then he hooked a chain to the car and pulled it out with his four-wheel-drive. He escorted us back across those thirty-two miles, waved us on after accepting our many thanks, and we traveled on good road the rest of the way to my parents' ranch.

We were a sorry sight to behold when we drove up the canyon to the ranch an hour later. Our parents were shocked and upset on hearing what had happened to us. Though we had told the Smacks we were coming, we hadn't been clear enough about when to expect us. My mother took Linda and my children to care for them. Our dear friend, Rita Smack, took my baby to bathe her and get all the dust out of her eyes, ears, and nose. I was so stiff and sore I thought I'd never be the same again. In his wisdom, Dad put me in his pickup and took me back down the canyon thirteen miles to Murphy's Hot Springs to take a hot mineral bath and soak some of the soreness out of my aching body. That helped me immensely, as did returning to all the comforts of the home I loved so much. I was home again with those I loved. But I got there on the "road less traveled by, and that has made all the difference."

This experience totally changed my perspective of many

things pertaining to life and its purpose. I learned much about faith and myself. I was indeed tutored by the Lord on the process and power of prayer. I learned as never before that trials and hardship are but tools and stepping stones to make us strong and teachable and willing to rely on the Lord for the help we need.

As children of God, we are all "homeward bound," and we all need each other. The path is marked, the way is set, the road is straight and narrow; we have a road map and directions by his word. We cannot get there without him. If we will seek a relationship with him, follow his example by obedience, rely on him as a source of strength and light with determination and faith, we will reach our home with him again. What a glorious reunion awaits us there!

I have set before you life and death, blessing and cursing:
therefore choose life, that both thou and thy seed may live.

DEUTERONOMY 30:19

IT FELT LIKE WALKING INTO A WALL
MICHAEL EARL

As I was driving along a deserted road one day, I saw what looked like a two-foot spool of rope. I thought it might be 200 to 300 feet of climbing rope and stopped my truck to take a closer look. I noticed that next to the spool was a box full of what looked like toilet paper rolls. As I walked toward the spool of rope, I saw the words "Primer Cord" written on the end of it. Primer cord is used as a fuse for explosives. It was then that I realized the accompanying box was full of dynamite!

I was very curious and thought seriously about taking the primer cord and dynamite home with me. Then I decided that it might be dangerous; explosives are often quite unstable. As I was toying with the idea I took a step closer—but it was almost like walking into a wall. I felt restrained by some unseen power.

I should have taken that sense of restraint as a clear indication that I should leave it alone, but instead my curiosity grew even greater. Even if I left the dynamite, I thought, at least I could use the primer cord. I took another step. I then experienced a strange sensation. It seemed like I was simultaneously drawn toward the explosives and still powerfully restrained. I have never in my life felt such a clear contrast between what seemed to be the power of good and evil, each pulling equally against me. With such equal and opposing forces working on me, I felt that I alone could make the decision, right or wrong. Would I follow my own desires to pick up the primer cord and take it home? Or would I heed the warning to leave it alone?

I am honest to say it was a struggle—the temptation to pick up that primer cord was real. But I didn't do it. I turned and got back into my truck. As I drove away I felt deeply relieved, and the Spirit bore witness that I had made the right decision. To this day, I wonder what would have happened to me, or possibly my family, if I had taken the primer cord or the dynamite. I continue to be very thankful for the Spirit of the Lord and its protective promptings.

The Lord our God did visit us with assurances . . .
[and] did speak peace to our souls.

—ALMA 58:11

A WARMTH WASHED OVER ME
JUDY TAYLOR YOUNG

Recently I had to go to the clinic for my regular mammo-gram. I was surprised to see that the clinic had hired a new technician—a man who is a member of my ward! He was the employee assigned to take down all my information and fill out my form. I don't know him well, but we do see each other every Sunday. It made me very uncomfortable to have to tell him a number of very personal things as he filled out the form. He was professional and always appropriate, but the form itself required that he ask me questions I didn't want to answer.

The next Sunday was fast Sunday. I was still feeling uncom-fortable and was prepared to avoid this brother if I saw him. Then, as the meeting progressed, I saw him stand and move up to the pulpit. "I don't know why I'm up here," he said. "But I just had an undeniable impression that it was important for me to bear my testimony today." He did so, and the spirit about him was sweet and good.

As he spoke, a warmth and peace washed over me. All my discomfort was gone. I'm grateful the Lord loves us and watches over us even in such little things as this.

And they did rejoice and cry again with one voice, saying:
May the God of Abraham, and the God of Isaac,
and the God of Jacob, protect this people
in righteousness, so long as they shall call on
the name of their God for protection.

3 NEPHI 4:30

A NIGHT OF FIRES
GEORGE C. THORDERSEN

One summer we took our family to Yellowstone Park for a vacation. We rented a small cabin in West Yellowstone where we stayed at night; then we traveled into the park each day. Our whole family was there except for one teenage son, whom we had allowed to stay at home for work. He was struggling with his values and had many rowdy friends. We were concerned about leaving him, but he promised to behave himself and not to have any parties at our home while we were gone.

On the third night of our trip I was awakened by a troubling dream that our house was on fire. I discovered that my wife was also awake—she had been disturbed by a dream that our house was on fire. We talked about it for a little while, then dozed off, only to be awakened by the same dream again.

We got up, knelt by the side of the bed, and pleaded for protection for our home. We had no telephone in the cabin and couldn't think of what else to do. After our prayer we felt a peaceful reassurance that the Lord would provide the protection we sought. We went back to bed and slept well for the rest of the night.

The next morning we packed up our family and headed home. When we arrived the house was still standing. But when we went inside we discovered that there had been a party at our home. We counted more than eighty beer cans in the house; one wall was full of dart holes—and there was evidence of fires. We found five separate locations where fires had been started but then had burned out, seemingly by themselves.

We learned that our teenage son had been at work when the "party" had occurred. He had known nothing of it and was genuinely upset when he learned what had happened.

We felt greatly blessed for the peace we gained from our prayers, and blessed for the help we received that reached beyond earthly powers.

*Have faith in God. For . . . whosoever . . . shall not doubt in his
heart, but shall believe that those things which he saith shall come
to pass; he shall have whatsoever he saith.*

MARK 11:22–23

"DO YOU REMEMBER
THE PROMISES YOU MADE?"
FREDERICK W. BABBEL

After [one meeting in postwar Germany] one sister came up
to me and asked, "Do you remember me?"

I looked searchingly at her and then replied, "You are Sister
Frenzel."

She confirmed this, then continued: "Do you remember the
promises you made to me when you blessed me just before you left
Nuremberg in 1939 to return home?"

How could I ever forget! I had given my farewell talk in
church. Then, by request, I went to her home to give her a blessing.
She was expecting her first child. Her health was so poor that she
had been unable to come to church except on rare occasions.
Because of serious physical complications and the fact that she
was in her forties while expecting this, her first child, the family

doctor had expressed grave concern that she might lose her own life in giving birth to a child.

In view of these problems she had asked for a special blessing.

Her husband was a cripple with one leg. They were poor people and lived in a little shed on their "Gartenlaube." This shed was ordinarily used to store garden tools, etc. for taking care of this little piece of land on which they might grow a few fruits and vegetables. Because of their meager circumstances, they had converted this into a one-room home. And under such circumstances the arrival of a child would be even more critical.

In the middle of the blessing I stopped, completely bewildered by the fact that I had blessed her that she would have a son. Knowing how literally these good people accepted every word of the leaders, I was concerned that I had committed a serious mistake.

My companion nudged me to go on. As I did so, I tried to think of how I could possibly word the blessing to make this a conditional promise. Then I realized that I had just said for a second time that her child should grow up to receive the priesthood and become a leader in the Church. At this point I recognized that I had left no room for retreat, so I resolved to continue the blessing and get through it as best I could.

To make matters even worse, as the blessing continued I promised her that she should have no serious pain in childbirth (yet her doctor feared for her very life) and that because of her faith she should yet rear a large family (this, too, was impossible, according to the doctor, who marveled that she could expect even one child because of her age.)

When the blessing had been concluded, she smiled and said, in effect, that she knew she would be all right, that she would have a son and that the Lord would bless and sustain her. Yes, how well I remember that blessing!

On my way home that evening, even the mission president had offered me no consolation. As I recounted the circumstances to him, he merely said, "You have a fifty-fifty chance of being right!"

It was now nearly seven years later. After my vivid split-second review, Sister Frenzel said to me, "I would like to have you meet my family." She then paraded her little ones before me— four or five of them, as I recall—and introduced them. Her first-born, a son, she had named Frederick William after me!

Another young man in the audience approached me a few moments later and asked, "Do you remember the promises you made to me when you blessed me just as I was entering the German Army?"

Again I recalled the circumstances rather vividly, and replied: "I believe I do. Why do you ask?"

"Because I have found the young woman I would like to marry. Do you think it is still possible for me to be married to her in the temple, as I was promised in that blessing?"

(I had promised him, according to his wishes, that if he lived a clean, pure life, the Lord would grant him the privilege of being married in the House of the Lord—a thing which seemed remote and impossible at that time when we were standing on the brink of the outbreak of World War II and he was going into the German infantry.)

As I looked upon his emaciated body—possibly weighing around 100 pounds instead of the 180 pounds or so he weighed when he entered the service—and realized the difficult circumstances under which he and many others lived, I became somewhat apprehensive. "Hans," I asked, "have you kept yourself morally clean since that day?"

"Yes, I have," he assured me. "I was severely wounded and left for dead on the battlefield more than once, but I have kept myself morally clean."

Then I was impressed to say: "Hans, if you have kept yourself clean and you still desire to make that promise a reality, claim your blessing from the Lord. I don't understand right now how it will be possible, but somehow the Lord will open the way."

(After I had returned home and was working in the Church Office Building in Salt Lake City, who should walk in one day but Hans and his sweetheart. They were being married in the temple. They had arranged for a visitor's visa and were to return to their homeland after their marriage and a short stay in the United States. How they were able to get the finances together to make this nearly fifteen-thousand-mile trip I do not know. I could not help marveling at the faith of that young man and his sweetheart.)

Babbel, *On Wings of Faith*, 63–64. Used by Permission.

If any of you lack wisdom, let him ask of God, that giveth to all men liberally, and upbraideth not; and it shall be given him. But let him ask in faith, nothing wavering.

JAMES 1:5–6

ONE CHANCE AT LAW SCHOOL
WENDY D. YOUNG

When my husband, Rob, was attending BYU he majored in electrical engineering. During his senior year a recruiter for patent attorneys for law school made a presentation in one of his classes. That opened up a whole new area of possibility for Rob. In the days that followed he and I talked through some of the options for his immediate future: law school, work, graduate school, and so forth. We both felt the most excitement about the idea of law school.

The more we prayed for guidance and looked at law school, the better we felt. We started looking up the requirements and locations of schools that had a good reputation for patent law. As we researched and continued to pray, we felt we should apply to Columbia Law School in New York. No other possibility felt right to us.

Because we were late in deciding about law school, Rob had only one chance to take the LSAT (Law School Admissions

Test)—making it a one-shot deal. He had a fairly average GPA and knew he had to do very well on the LSAT to make it into law school. He studied and prepared as well as possible in the short amount of time he could squeeze in between his regular classwork and other responsibilities. He prayed that if it was Heavenly Father's will he might be able to do well on the test. He took the test and did indeed do very well, which gave him some hope that he could actually be accepted into law school. We were encouraged to learn, after feeling that Columbia was the place to go, that they relied more on the LSAT score than on an undergraduate GPA.

After Rob took the LSAT, we were faced with a dilemma. It seemed unwise to apply to only one law school—what if they turned him down? On the other hand, each application took money that we didn't have. And we didn't feel like there was any point in applying at any school besides Columbia, because we felt Columbia was the place we were supposed to go. After further prayer, we decided we should put all our eggs in one basket. Rob applied to Columbia, and nowhere else, and we left the result in the hands of the Lord—while continuing to pray for his help.

In February we were sent word that we had been accepted to be on the waiting list at Columbia. We cheered, then renewed our prayers, asking that if it was indeed the Lord's will, we would be able to be fully accepted. We waited anxiously for each cut and each time received word that we were still on the waiting list. Then, only five days before orientation, we received a phone call that we had been accepted. Our prayers had been answered!

We hurriedly packed our things into a U-Haul and drove to New York with our two-year-old baby. We didn't have a place to live, we didn't have money to pay for school, and we had little money for our living expenses. But we knew that if we were truly doing Heavenly Father's will he would help us to survive. We have had some significant hardships and trials—which continue as we are cramped into a small living space with an active two year old—but we know that all will be well. The Lord is with us, and as long as we are obedient and rely on him, he will see us through.

And Elijah said unto her, . . . thus saith the Lord God of Israel,
The barrel of meal shall not waste, neither shall the cruse of oil fail,
until the day that the Lord sendeth rain upon the earth.

1 KINGS 17:13–14

ONE SHOVELFUL OF COAL
MARJORIE A. McCORMICK

World War II had been over for almost two years, but we were still on rations.

It was February 1947, one of the hardest winters anyone could remember. Our hometown of Bradford, Yorkshire, England, was the coldest spot in the nation, and it had snowed off and on for six weeks.

By now the drifted snow was higher than our heads—that meant no cart could reach us to deliver our ration of coal. And we were running low.

There were six of us living together that winter—my husband and I, our two children, a young man who had been turned out of his own home when he joined the Church, and a woman whose daughter was serving a mission. We did our best to keep warm, but we were almost out of fuel and we only had electricity at certain hours during the day. (Most of our power stations had been badly bombed during the war.)

It was Saturday when my husband went down to the cellar and carefully sifted the coal from the dust. All that remained was one shovelful of coal and a few cans of coal dust.

At church the next day, we received a shopping bag full of wood. The elders had sawed the wood from old railroad ties and stored it in the basement of the church. With this wood and our little pile of coal, we had fuel enough for one more day.

That evening we knelt in prayer and asked the Lord to help us. As we prayed, our helplessness gave way to a sense of peace. When we went to bed, we felt content to leave the situation in the Lord's hands.

On Monday morning I put some wood, a can of dust, and the remaining coal into the fireplace. Then I waited until afternoon to start the fire—I wanted the house to be as warm as possible when the children got home from school.

The fire lasted until nine or ten that night. We were amazed to discover that all six of us kept warm and comfortable from the one little fire through the entire evening. My husband added a can of dust and one log, but that was all.

The next morning I cleaned out the fireplace and began to lay paper and wood as I had the day before. Then I plucked up my courage and faith and went down to the cellar. Not knowing quite what to expect, I opened the door. There, in the same corner where it had been yesterday, was a stack of coal that looked just like the coal we had burned the night before. I had the strangest feeling—had an angel brought it? I had no answer for my question, but I reverently scooped up the coal and took it upstairs.

How grateful we were that night for our miraculous fire. Our prayers were prayers of appreciation and praise.

The next morning when I went down to the cellar I found another stack of coal in the same corner. It was just enough. This miracle occurred every day that week until Saturday. By that time my husband felt that the snow had melted enough so that he would finally be able to get us some coal.

He took the children's sled, and as soon as he left I went down to the cellar. As soon as I saw the corner I knew that he would bring back some coal; there was no coal in the cellar.

Later that day my husband brought back two lovely hundred-weight sacks of coal.

I still have no explanation for this incident. All I know is that it did happen and six of us witnessed it. And we know that God lives and answers prayers.

"One Shovelful of Coal." Marjorie A. McCormick. Previously published in the Ensign October 1979, 49–50. © by Intellectual Reserve, Inc. Used by permission.

SOURCES

Anderson, Dawn Hall, Dlora Dalton Hall, and Susette Fletcher Green, eds. *Every Good Thing: Talks from the 1997 Women's Conference*. Salt Lake City: Deseret Book, 1998.

Anderson, Leland E. *Stories of Power and Purpose*. Salt Lake City: Bookcraft, 1974.

Ayres, Kendall, ed. *Great Teaching Moments*. Salt Lake City: Bookcraft, 1990.

Babbel, Frederick W. *On Wings of Faith*. Salt Lake City: Bookcraft, 1972.

Burgess, Allan K., and Max H. Molgard. *Stories That Teach Gospel Principles*. Salt Lake City: Bookcraft, 1989.

Goddard, Wallace H., and Richard H. Cracroft, eds. *My Soul Delighteth in the Scriptures: Personal and Family Applications*. Salt Lake City: Bookcraft, 1999.

Jensen, Margie C., comp. *Stories of Insight and Inspiration*. Salt Lake City: Bookcraft, 1976.

———. *When Faith Writes the Story*. Salt Lake City: Bookcraft, 1973.

Kapp, Ardeth G. *The Joy of the Journey.* Salt Lake City: Deseret Book, 1992.

Purser, John. "Testimony of John and Donna Purser," 8 September 1964. In *The Builders Testify,* comp. Doris Taggart. Typescript. Salt Lake City: Utah: n.p., 1965?. Available in Archives, Church Historical Department, The Church of Jesus Christ of Latter-day Saints.

Rasmus, Carolyn J. *In the Strength of the Lord I Can Do All Things.* Salt Lake City: Deseret Book, 1990.

Thy Word Is a Lamp: Women's Stories of Finding Light. Salt Lake City: Deseret Book, 1999.

SCRIPTURE INDEX

OLD TESTAMENT

Deuteronomy
30:19, p. 185

1 Kings
17:13–14, p. 198

2 Kings
19:20, p. 119

Psalms
36:7, p. 95
55:22, p. 42
81:7, p. 127
145:20, p. 167
147:2–3, p. 124

Proverbs
3:5–6, p. 155
16:20, p. 27
30:5, p. 132

Ecclesiastes
11:1, p. 1

Isaiah
40:29, 31, p. 170
41:13, p. 135, p. 167
46:4, p. 60
58:13–14, p. 77

Joel
2:32, p. 45

NEW TESTAMENT

Matthew
9:22, p. 140
10:39, p. 98
25:40, p. 12

Mark
11:22–23, p. 191

Luke
6:38, p. 143
9:16–17, p. 38

1 Corinthians
13:4–5, p. 4

James
1:5–6, p. 195
5:14–15, p. 114
5:16, p. 9

BOOK OF MORMON

1 Nephi
4:6, p. 117
17:3, p. 6
17:13, p. 101

17:45, p. 153

2 Nephi
4:19–20, p. 50
26:15, p. 151

Jacob
3:1, p. 21

Enos
1:9, p. 67
1:10, p. 92

Mosiah
5:2, p. 138
24:15, p. 88
27:30, p. 15

Alma
5:12, p. 33
7:12, p. 84
7:23, p. 129
12:34, p. 80
20:4, p. 58
31:33–34, p. 69

33:5, p. 164
37:37, p. 55
58:11, p. 187

3 Nephi
4:30, p. 189

Ether
12:27, p. 105

Moroni
10:4, p. 112

DOCTRINE AND COVENANTS

6:22–23, p. 107
18:34–36, p. 52
39:10, p. 23
58:4, p. 74
61:36, p. 146
84:46, p. 17
88:64, p. 62
104:80, p. 31
112:10, p. 40
121:45, p. 148

INDEX

Aarons, J. C., 117
accident, 141: suffered by
    missionary, 107; auto, 114, 172;
    household, 156
Adams, Peter C., 119
adversity, 119–22, 125
afflictions, ability to endure, xiv
agency, 52–54, 84; unwise use of,
    80–83
Air National Guard, 119–23
Alma, missionary labors of, 72–73
Anderson, Leland E., 9
anger: overcoming, 5, 35, 138–39; at
    God, 67
anointing of the sick, 114, 117–18.
    See also priesthood blessings
answers, recognizing, 113. *See also*
    prayer
Asay, Jean, 52
Atonement, power of the, 44. *See
    also* Jesus Christ
attitude, 139; toward family
    members, 4–5; toward service,
    14; change of, 43–44, 71–72,
    90–91, 159; of missionary, 67–68;
    judgmental, 148–50

Babbel, Frederick W., 124, 191
Ballif-Spanvill, Bonnie, 129

Barrowes, Dee Ann, 50
Barrowes, Orlando T., 127
Berlin Wall, 46
bishop, counsel given by, 42
bishopric, selecting member of,
    40–41
Black, Julie Stinson, 21
blessings, 163; financial, 74–76,
    78–79; to families of
    missionaries, 110; material,
    144–45, 162, 199
Book of Mormon, gaining testimony
    of, 24–26
Brandt, Dieter, 45
burdens: bearing others', 42–44;
    lifting of, 84–87; ability to bear,
    89–90
Burgess, Allan K., 98

career, 95–97
celebrations, family, 164
challenges, financial, 61, 78, 89, 95
Channell, R. Reed, 40
chapel, building of, 38
charity: acts of, 14, 28, 61, 143–45;
    gift of, 149
childbirth, 151–52, 191–92;
    inspiration regarding, 60–61
children: caring for, 58–59;

wayward, 84–87; prayers of, 127–28; physical needs of, 174

choice and accountability, 10, 52–54, 80–81, 84, 133

Church callings, 40–41, 136, 142; receiving inspiration in, 12–15, 42–44

Church Educational System, 69–70

Church membership, preparation for, 17–20

Church welfare program, 1

Church work, God's hand in, 38–39

Clark, Thomas R., 161

comfort, from Spirit, 187. *See also* Holy Ghost

commitment, to serve mission, 7–8

communism, 46–49

contention, 34

conversion, 17–20; of Uruguayan family, 23

counsel, parental, 138–39

courtship, 46

Cracroft, Richard H., 101

criticism, 148

curiosity, 185–86

Cutler, Carma N., 1

danger: in nature, 127–28, 140–41, 167–68; avoiding, 134

dating, 52–54

death: of parents, 6, 98, 146; of children, 125; of family members, 129, 170; eternal perspective on, 130

decisions, 52–54

delegation, 13

depression, 86, 98–99, 129

desires, righteous, 129–30

despair, 125–26

determination, 174–80

Dick, Lauren A., 107

disability, 76

discipline problems, 72

discouragement: of missionary, 27–28; in family history work, 63–64; overcoming, 180

doubt, overcoming, 25, 109

dreams, and inspiration, 189

drug addiction, 15, 81–83, 85–86

dyslexia, 55–57

Eardley, Roscoe, 9

Earl, Michael, 185

East Prussia, 124

education, 55–57, 135, 195

emergencies, 58–59, 146–47

Enos, example of, 67–68

example: power of, 30; setting an, 120

exhaustion, 34

expectations, parental, 85

faith, 25, 87, 101, 140–42; miracles wrought by, xv–xvi; setting example of, 29–30; in inspiration, 57, 94, 109, 153–54, 165–66; in God's promises, 100; to find lost object, 101–4; of student, 136–37; of expectant parents, 151–52; in priesthood blessings, 193

family history work, 62–66, 153–54

family: protection of, 31–32; challenges regarding, 33–37;

inspiration regarding, 60–61; loss of, 129, 170; closeness to, 161–63; examples in, 179

family prayer, 190

fasting and prayer, 17; for sustenance, 7–8; for children's welfare, 56; regarding family history work, 65; regarding job, 74; for spiritual progress, 106; for expectant mother, 151

fatigue, 34

fear: overcoming, 110–11, 159–160; calmed by prayer, 127–28

fellowshipping, 10–11

Fenstermaker, Suzanne, 95

financial blessings: sacrifice followed by, 2; for missionary, 8

Ford, Tandea, 112

forgiveness, 35, 83; of parent, 5

friends, influence of, 80–81

friendship, building, 70

genealogy, 66, 153–54

Germany, 191; East and West, 45–49

gifts, spiritual, 64

Giles, Christie Ann, 67

God: love of, xiv; children of, 21–22, 149–50; reliance on, 41, 177, 197; submission to will of, 90, 130, 142; ways of, 101; wisdom of, 118; trust in, 158–59

grandparents, 170

gratitude, 152; for small blessings, 104, 166, 188; for protection, 157, 169; for material blessings, 200

Greenhalgh, Garrick, 27

grief, 125, 129, 170

Griffin, Tracey, 138

guidance: of Holy Ghost, 32; seeking the Lord's, 105–6; prayer for, 175; in educational goals, 195

habits, overcoming, 15–16, 138–39, 148–50

happiness, xiii, 29–30; seeking, 34, 98–100; through service, 99; in adversity, 126

hardship, enduring, 146–47, 184

healing, 51, 140–42; of missionary, 107–11

health, 61; care, 50–51, 74–76, 93–94; concerns, 74–76, 191–92; of mother and baby, 151–52

heart: change of, 67–68, 138–39; softening of, 72–73; pure in, 123

Heavenly Father: as teacher, 34–37; burdens lifted by, 43–44; patience of, 94; communication with, 113; reliance on, 139, 145; perspective of, 150. See also God

Heiner, Ruth, 77

high school students, teaching, 69–70

Hinckley, Marjorie Pay, on small miracles, xvii

Hofheins, Joan Lloyd, 62

Holbrook, David C., 42

Holy Ghost: guidance by, 9, 32, 47–48; nonmember inspired by, 17–20; as teacher, 20, 34–37, 168–69; bishop inspired by, 40–41; parents taught by, 49–56;

family history inspired by, 64; as comforter, 86–87, 108, 147, 187–88; warnings of, 133, 174–75; whisperings of, 153–54, 161; receiving confirmation from, 176
home, 161–63
hope, 29–30, 86–87
hostility, toward Church member, 135
humility: seeking, 106; in wartime, 125
humor, 3
hymns, 29–30, 108–9

illness, 74–76, 157–58; long-term, 50–51, 98; of parent, 92
Indian Placement Program, 143
individual worth, 21–22
influences, unwholesome, 9–11, 80–81, 119, 133
injury, 141; protection from, 59; serious, 115, 117
inspiration, xiii, 21–22, 133, 165; in relationships, 4–5; on needs of others, 9, 171; in Church callings, 12, 40–41; on life's direction, 17–18; preparation to receive, 18; heeding, 48–49, 93–94, 103–4, 137, 162; in parenting, 53, 55–59, 87; in family history work, 62–66, 153–54; on career, 97; on happiness, 99; understanding meaning of, 109, 113; on God's will, 129–30; on personal safety, 168; accepting, 192, 196

instability, financial, 95–96
intelligence, flashes of, 103
Iron Curtain, 45–49
Isaacson, Rebekah, 105

Jared, brother of, 101–2
Jensen, Jay E., on identifying the Spirit, xvi
Jesus Christ: mighty miracles of, xi; atonement of, 5, 21–22, 35, 83; belief in, 126
job: 95–97; loss of, 74–76, 95–97
Jolie, Tamara, 146
Jones, Eva Dawn, 55
joy, as gift from God, 36–37

Kapp, Ardeth G., 15
Keiser, Cindee, 31
Kimball, Spencer W., on modern-day miracles, xv-xvi
King, Samuel, 23–26

learning disabilities, 55–59
Lee, Harold B., 133–34; on seeking guidance, 101
Lee, Jenna, 164
light: of Christ, 18–19; walking to edge of, 101
Lindstrom, Joyce, 153
London, Brett G., 135
love: God's, 15–16, 87; for students, 71–72; for family member, 147

Mahonri Moriancumer, 101–2
mankind, God's love for, 15–16
Markham, John W., 92
marriage, 33–34; temple, 193–94

Maxwell, Neal A., 86; on "divine discontent," 149

McConkie, Bruce R., on the light of Christ, 19

McCormick, Marjorie A., 198

meditation, 71

member missionaries, 10, 121

members, less active, 15–16, 80–81

military service, 119–23

Millet, Robert L., 69

miracles, 38–39; mighty, xi; modern-day, xv-xvi; small, 3; faith and, 101–2; of healing, 110–11

missionary: inspiration received by, 20; healing of, 107–11

missionary experiences, 101–4

Missionary Training Center (MTC), 67

missionary work, 23–30, 67–68; commitment to, 6–8; in military service, 121;

Molgard, Max H., 98

Montevideo, Uruguay, 23

Moses, miracles performed by, xi

mother: prayer of, 11; as example, 98

motherhood, 95–97, 125, 138–39, 151–52; challenges of, 33–37; and career, 88–91, 95–97

Mount Timpanogos, 127–28

music, power of, 29–30, 177

"myths," Mormon, xviii

needs, temporal, 199

neighbor, developing love for, 148–50

New York City, 132

obedience, 121, 143, 197; to inspiration, 47–49, 101–4, 133; to law of Sabbath, 77–79

opposition, 185–86

oppression, communist, 47–49

Packer, Boyd K., on teaching, 70

pain, physical, 93–94, 181

parent, death of, 98

parenting, 96, 155, 164–66; of teenagers, 52–54; inspiration in, 59; challenges of, 84–87, 138–39

parents: death of, 6, 146; responsibility to, 94

Parry, Atwell J., 140

patience, 4–5, 70; in waiting for answers, 106

patriarchal blessings, 86, 88

peace: inner, 33–37, 44, 108, 131; in trials, 86–87

Perkes, Alden, 132

persecution, 29

personal progress, 105

Philippines, missionary work in, 27–30

physical strength, 176–80

Pierce, Jody Higham, 33

polio, 50–51

pondering, 71

popularity, 122

poverty, 28; in wartime, 124, 198

prayer, 51, 120, 183; for courage, 13–14, 126, 128; for safety, 31–32, 47, 168, 175; for change of heart, 35; for ward members, 44; for sick spouse, 50–51, 129; for strength, 59; in parenting,

60–61; in family history work, 64; insincere, 67; to change others, 70–71; for charity, 71–72; answers to, 87, 104, 113, 130–31; for material blessings, 96, 144, 162; for help, 103, 173; to accept God's will, 107; for strength of character, 122; of child, 127–28; for patience, 138–39; for guidance, 149, 153–54, 164–65, 196–97; for understanding, 158; family, 190; regarding educational goals, 196–97

preparation, for answers to prayer, 196

pride, overcoming, 35, 106

priesthood: gratitude for, 83; power of the, 115–16

priesthood blessings: for guidance, 82, 191; for peace, 90, 129–30; for healing, 114, 117, 142; for increased faith, 159

priorities, 89, 136–37, 155

promises: in priesthood blessing, 192; fulfillment of, 193–94

protection, 59, 185–86; from evil, 9–11; of family members, 31–32; of home, 190

Purser, John, 38

Rasmus, Carolyn J., 17–20

Rasmussen, Blaine, 58

Rawson, Emily J., 4

Reading, Neal, 102–3

reassurance, through prayer, 190

records, translation of, 64–66

refugees, 124–25

relationships, family, 4–5, 33

reliance, on God, 177

relief, 183

repentance, 35–36, 43–44, 71–72, 82–83

reputation, 122

resources, multiplied by the Lord, 38–39

Ririe, R. Samuel, 60

Sabbath day observance, 77–79, 121, 136

sacrifice, 143; blessings of, 2

safety, personal, 140–41

Sandberg, Darlene, 84

Sandberg, Trevor, 80

scripture study, 113

scriptures: promises in, xii-xiii; receiving inspiration through, 14, 25, 112; receiving guidance through, 53, 72–73, 89–90; missionary guided by, 67–68; examples found in, 101–2, 144; seeking guidance in, 160

self-doubt, 85

self-pity, 99

self-sacrifice, 99–100, 181

self-worth, 21–22

seminary, 69–73

service, 76; charitable, 1–3; blessings of, 3, 14; as antidote to self-pity, 99

sick, caring for the, 12–15

signs, belief followed by, xii-xiii

Smith, Joseph: gaining testimony of, 24–26; on "flashes of intelligence," 103

sorrow, 131, 170
Sowell, Richard T., 114
Spirit, identifying workings of, xvi.
    See also Holy Ghost
spiritual gifts, seeking, 64, 149
strength, mother blessed with, 158
strengths, developing, 106
submission, to will of God, 107, 130
success, academic, 57
sustenance, need for, 174

Taylor, JoAnn, 143
Taylor, Jon M., 167
Teach Ye Diligently, 70
teaching, 88–89; principles of,
    69–73
temper, controlling, 138–39
temple work, 63
temptation, xiii, 133–34, 185–86
testimony, 19–20, 24–26, 126; of
    Book of Mormon, 112–13;
    gained through trials, 180;
    sharing, 187
Thordersen, George C., 189
time management, 89, 136
tithing, 18
Tolman, Daniel A., 148
tribulations, enduring, 124–25,
    130–31

trust, 108, 145
truth, seeking, 112–13

unbelief, consequences of, xv
unemployment, 74–76

volunteerism, 76

Warr, LaRae, 77
Warr, Quinten, 77
weaknesses: recognizing, 105;
    overcoming, 149
Wight, Sarah Jane, 12
Williams, Brandon R., 151
Wilson, Margaret Barton, 170
wisdom, financial, 78
womanhood, 21–22, 155
Woods, Debra Sansing, 155
Word of Wisdom, 10, 19, 80–83,
    122
work, honest, 76
World War II, 124, 191, 198
worry, 42–44, 160, 175–76

Yellowstone Park, 167
YMMIA, 45–46
Young, Judy Taylor, 187
Young, Wendy D., 195

Zimmer, Max, 124

ABOUT THE AUTHOR

Jay A. Parry has worked as an editor for the *Ensign* magazine, as a freelance writer, and as an editor for Deseret Book.

Brother Parry has served in The Church of Jesus Christ of Latter-day Saints as a bishop, a high councilor, and as chair of a general Church curriculum writing committee.

A prolific writer, he has most recently published *Understanding the Signs of the Times, Understanding the Book of Revelation,* and *Understanding Isaiah* (all coauthored with Donald W. Parry). He is also one of the creators and compilers of the successful "Best-Loved" series, which includes *Best-Loved Stories of the LDS People* (three volumes), *Best-Loved Poems of the LDS People,* and *Best-Loved Humor of the LDS People.*

He and his wife, Vicki Hughes Parry, are the parents of seven children and have four granddaughters.